A Guide to Navigation for Young Adventurers

HOW TO GO ANYWHERE (AND NOT GET LOST)

HANS ASCHIM
ILLUSTRATED BY **ANDRÉS LOZANO**

WORKMAN PUBLISHING
NEW YORK

LIBRARY OF CONGRESS CATALOGING-IN-PUBLICATION DATA IS AVAILABLE.

ISBN 978-1-5235-0634-7

COVER AND ILLUSTRATIONS BY ANDRÉS LOZANO
DESIGN BY SARA CORBETT, JOOAHN KWON, JOHN PASSINEAU, AND MONIQUE STERLING

WORKMAN BOOKS ARE AVAILABLE AT SPECIAL DISCOUNTS WHEN PURCHASED
IN BULK FOR PREMIUMS AND SALES PROMOTIONS AS WELL AS FOR FUND-RAISING
OR EDUCATIONAL USE. SPECIAL EDITIONS OR BOOK EXCERPTS CAN ALSO BE
CREATED TO SPECIFICATION. FOR DETAILS, CONTACT THE SPECIAL SALES DIRECTOR
AT SPECIALMARKETS@WORKMAN.COM.

WORKMAN PUBLISHING CO., INC.
225 VARICK STREET
NEW YORK, NY 10014-4381
WORKMAN.COM

WORKMAN IS A REGISTERED TRADEMARK OF WORKMAN PUBLISHING CO., INC.

PRINTED IN CHINA
FIRST PRINTING FEBRUARY 2021

10 9 8 7 6 5 4 3 2 1

PHOTO CREDITS: Alamy: Art Directors & TRIP p. 97; B Christopher p. 190; Classic
Image p. 175; David Noton Photography p. 138; Digital Image Library p. 129; FLHC3 p. 93;
GoSeeFoto p. 158; Iconographic Archive p. 72; Inge Johnsson p. 177; National Geographic
Image Collection p. 31; North Wind Picture Archives p. 74; Ihor Svetiukha p. 162; The
History Collection p. 43; YAY Media AS p. 63. **Getty Images:** jodie coston/E+ p. 76; Eric
Ferguson/iStock p. 182; LOUISA GOULIAMAKI/AFP p. 71; Science Museum/SSPL
pp. 69, 70; ullstein bild p. 13; Universal History Archive/Universal Images Group p. 140.
Wikimedia Commons: Bordwall p. 73

For my parents,
who always encouraged me to go outside
and get lost. And still do.

★ ★ ★

EARTH AT A GLANCE

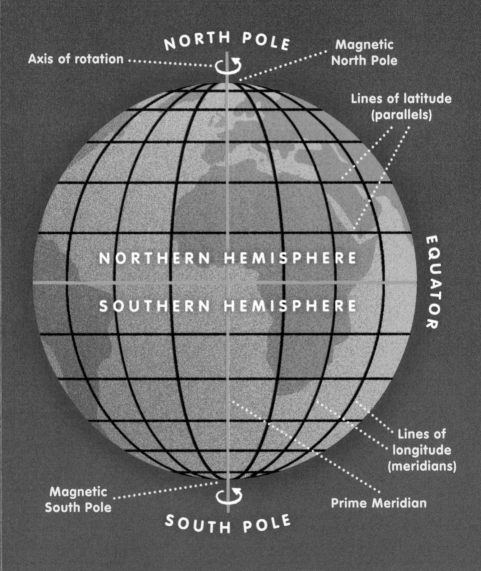

Axis of rotation · · · · · · · ·

NORTH POLE

Magnetic North Pole

Lines of latitude (parallels)

NORTHERN HEMISPHERE

SOUTHERN HEMISPHERE

EQUATOR

Lines of longitude (meridians)

Magnetic South Pole

SOUTH POLE

Prime Meridian

CONTENTS

THE HUMAN ART OF MOVING AROUND: A TIMELINE

70,000 YEARS AGO: *Homo sapiens* (human beings) begin migrating out of Africa. They aren't exactly navigating—more likely they are looking for food—but they are moving!

15,000 YEARS AGO: A group of seriously daring hunters reaches the Americas via the Bering Land Bridge and Kelp Highway.

4900 BCE: One of the earliest known sun calendars, the Goseck Circle, is created in present-day Germany.

3000 BCE: The Lapita people set sail from Southeast Asia to the South Pacific, settling in remote islands like Palau, Tonga, and Samoa.

1550 BCE: Shadow clocks are developed in ancient Egypt that later give way to sundials.

206 BCE–220 CE: The compass is invented in China. At first it is used for fortune-telling; centuries later, its navigation potential is harnessed on the high seas.

200 BCE: Ancient Greeks develop the first known astrolabe, a device used to read the angle of the sun and stars against the horizon.

700 CE: Polynesians refine their celestial navigation techniques, enabling them to traverse nearly 3,000 miles of ocean from Tahiti to Hawai'i.

800 CE: Arab navigators create the kamal, a device that helps sailors determine their latitude, or north-south position.

1400: Portuguese sailors slim down the astrolabe and make it more user-friendly at sea. The mariner's astrolabe helps usher in the Age of European Exploration that lasts from 1400 to about 1700.

1492: Italian explorer Christopher Columbus makes his fateful (if accidental) journey to the Americas.

1519: Ferdinand Magellan begins what we believe to be the first round-the-world trip (circumnavigation). His crew finishes without him in 1522 after he dies in the Philippines.

1761: The first clock capable of keeping time at sea (John Harrison's marine chronometer, H4) solves the problem of determining longitude, or east-west position.

1884: An international agreement is made to use Greenwich, England, as the Prime Meridian, standardizing time and east-west distance.

1901: Guglielmo Marconi sends the first wireless radio signals across the Atlantic Ocean, marking a new era of communication and navigation.

1930s: Networks of radio stations and onboard radio navigation make airplane travel safer and more efficient.

1957: The Soviet Union surprises the world with *Sputnik 1*, the first satellite sent into orbit.

1978: The United States launches Navstar GPS, a network of global positioning satellites.

2000: The full capability of GPS is made available to the public for free.

2019: Google Maps, the go-to GPS navigation app, surpasses one billion users.

FOREWORD

* * *

by Nainoa Thompson

Growing up in Hawai'i, I did my best learning in the ocean. I would fish on the reefs outside Honolulu and I quickly developed a close relationship with the sea. Those early experiences led me to sail across oceans in the traditional Hawaiian way, using only the stars and natural world around me as a guide. But first I had a lot to learn and there weren't many who could teach me.

Large portions of Hawaiian history, like our nautical wayfinding techniques, were erased when the Polynesian islands, including Hawai'i, were colonized. Wayfinding using traditional ways was more than an adventure, it was a way to renew the pride of my seafaring heritage.

The first time I was set to sail across the Pacific Ocean—from Tahiti to my home in Hawai'i—my teacher, Mau Piailug, backed out just before we pushed off. My crew and I were passionate but unexperienced sailors.

But Mau said we weren't ready for such a journey. I wouldn't see him again for three years. In the meantime, I studied, I worked, and I failed.

After returning to Hawai'i, I set out to learn as much as I possibly could about the movements of the stars and the moon. I carefully observed the patterns of ocean waves and the winds. I learned the migrations of the sea life below the surface and the birds' overhead. My crew put in work of their own. We sailed together as a team.

After two years of preparation, we again set out for Tahiti in our 62-foot double-hulled canoe called *Hōkūle'a*, named for the Hawaiian Star of Gladness. Our destination lay over 2,200 miles away. We soon hit rough weather and high seas and *Hōkūle'a* flipped. We clung to the slippery underside of the canoe's hull and launched flares. A close friend and crewmember, Eddie Aikau, who was also the first lifeguard in

Hawai'i, paddled away on a surfboard in the direction of shore to get help.

As night began to creep in, we were spotted and brought to safety. We were badly shaken. Despite a massive search, Eddie wasn't seen again. His pride in Polynesian culture and dream of sailing the old ways is part of what inspired me to not give up. I kept going, and I knew I needed to learn more. To be better prepared for the next journey, I needed my teacher.

Three years earlier, Mau Piailug had rightly said we weren't ready to navigate the seas in the traditional Polynesian way. Mau was perhaps the last living person with the traditional wayfinding knowledge. I tracked down Mau on his island home in Micronesia and my education began. Over the next two winters, Mau shared his knowledge with me.

In 1980, *Hōkūle'a* set sail for Tahiti once more. It was the first time in over a thousand years that Hawaiians navigated a boat thousands of miles without navigation instruments. Our journey emboldened the Hawaiian people to feel pride in their culture. It contributed to a resurgence in the Polynesian language and traditions that continue today.

Since that first journey, the Polynesian Voyaging Society has sailed *Hōkūleʻa* hundreds of thousands of miles around the world. We are spreading the art and science of traditional Polynesian voyaging while inspiring the spirit of exploration through education.

Embarking on an adventure doesn't require a double-hulled canoe and a wide-open ocean. Every time we set out to learn something new, we go on a journey. Learning from those who have come before us, like I did with Mau, can connect us both to our past and to the future. When we learn and share knowledge with others, we become a part of something much bigger than ourselves. So, take on this challenge to learn, go on your own voyage, and share what you learn along the way.

Nainoa Thompson is the president of the Polynesian Voyaging Society and a Pwo navigator.

AUTHOR'S NOTE

★ ★ ★

When I decided to write this book, writing was the last thing a responsible person should have been thinking about. I was all alone 3 miles (4.8km) off the coast of Maui, bobbing around in house-size ocean waves (known as swells) with an 11-foot (3.4m) paddle board that suddenly felt like a cork. The cliffs disappeared with the roll of each swell—then I was even more alone, sandwiched in the alleyway of neighboring two-story waves.

Soon the cliffs on shore disappeared altogether. Instead of panicking, I started getting curious. How did anyone ever figure out how to navigate this crazy planet? All I could think about was how people set sail out into this same ocean with nothing but their knowledge of the world around them.

I was in Hawai'i reporting on a big wave surfing event for a national magazine. Having grown up on the Great Lakes, I was no stranger to spending time on the water in rough weather. But this was different. I couldn't tell one seemingly identical patch of sea apart from the next. The rolling of the swell made it hard to even think straight.

Then, luckily, an outrigger canoe crested over a swell. The paddler up front nodded casually in the direction of land like he was giving directions to a restaurant. I made it back to shore after two hours of hard paddling and a lot of thinking.

★ ★ ★

The story of navigation is the story of human history. Since the beginning, we've always moved around, whether it's for more space, more food, or natural curiosity. But navigation is a tool, and like any tool, it can be used to help or harm, to create or destroy. Advancements in navigation have given rise to some of the most destructive periods of history. Their effects are still felt today.

Starting in the 1400s, seafaring European countries used global exploration to create colonial empires. They wreaked havoc around the world for their profit. For centuries, millions of Africans were enslaved and brought to the New World in the transatlantic slave trade. Entire communities of Indigenous peoples have been destroyed, their cultures erased.

At the same time, navigation can enrich us. The movement of people also allows for the exchange of ideas and the creation of unique cultures. But how did we get here? Before there was any faint idea of the technology we rely on today, how did people move around? How did their methods vary across cultures? And why does it still matter?

Over the following six chapters we'll explore these questions and learn some seriously useful skills. We'll cover everything from looking at a tree and finding north, to using the stars to tell time, to locating Global Positioning System (GPS) routes.

Navigators have always relied on observation of clues beyond their location to know where they're heading. By learning observation skills and different means of navigation, we can not only learn more about the world around us but also enjoy the journey. And if we read closely, we'll be able to go anywhere and not get lost.

—Hans Aschim

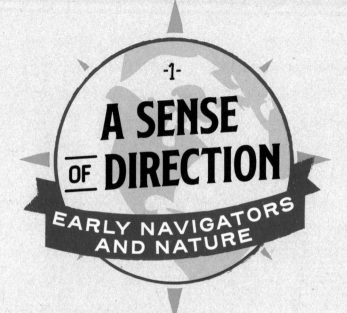

-1-
A SENSE OF DIRECTION

EARLY NAVIGATORS AND NATURE

What comes to mind when you think of navigation? For most of us it's all of the nifty gadgets used over the ages to explore the world. There are pirate compasses embedded with diamonds, or those storybook-like maps from the Age of European Exploration (which lasted from about 1400 to 1700) with sea monsters drawn in the unknown corners. Or maybe it's powerful modern GPS devices that can pinpoint your location to within inches using satellites.

But we risk-loving humans didn't just discover compasses buried in the ground or get lucky when we drew maps.

We had to figure it out over centuries of observation, persistence, and ingenuity. Early navigators used the sun, stars, and clues from nature to find their way— but it wasn't easy. We did it using good old-fashioned (*really* old-fashioned) trial and error. In other words, we got lost. A lot.

Early navigators had no way of being sure where they were going (or really where they were starting from). It took some serious courage to leave home with little certainty of coming back and almost no idea of where you were headed. But the adventure and opportunities were too much to resist.

HUMANS: BORN TO EXPLORE

Fresh air, some new company, and a kitchen restock are some of the reasons early navigators left the comforts of home for the great unknown—though they were tracking herds of woolly mammoths rather than picking up groceries down the block. In fact, the history of moving around for food, land, wealth, or ideas dates back to the early days of humanity itself. Archaeologists, paleontologists, and historians can't seem to totally agree on exactly who settled what, where, and when, but we do know a few things. The earliest fossil evidence of *Homo sapiens* (hey, that's us!) dates back to around 300,000 years ago and was found in Morocco.

For the next 230,000-odd years humans were content to hang out in Africa, spreading mostly to the lush lakes, fertile river valleys, and abundant coasts. We humans are a curious bunch, however, and eventually we got itchy feet. The first *Homo sapiens* arrived in Asia around 70,000 years ago and from there would head south, island-hopping down to what are now Indonesia and Australia. About 50,000 years ago we ventured into the deserts of the Middle East and Central Asia.

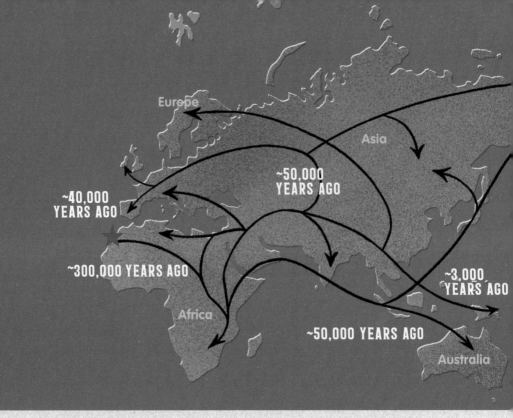

Europe

Asia

~50,000 YEARS AGO

~40,000 YEARS AGO

~300,000 YEARS AGO

~3,000 YEARS AGO

Africa

~50,000 YEARS AGO

Australia

Humans reached Europe about 40,000 years ago, some traveling along the Mediterranean coast while other groups cruised along the Danube River from the Black Sea. The Americas (that's everything from the top of Canada to the southern tip of Argentina) were the final continents to be settled by humans, some 25,000 years ago. Antarctica is the only continent on Earth without an indigenous (native-born) population. But our coldest, windiest, and southernmost continent is home to a group of scientists and researchers from around the world that peaks at just 5,000 in the summer months.

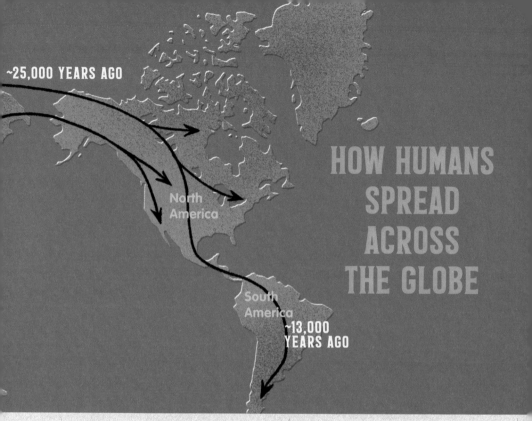

~25,000 YEARS AGO

HOW HUMANS
SPREAD
ACROSS
THE GLOBE

North
America

South
America

~13,000
YEARS AGO

Until recently, experts thought all would-be Americans arrived via a 2,000-mile-long (3,219km) land bridge that connected Siberia (in Asia) to Alaska (in North America). While some intrepid travelers took that Bering Land Bridge route, new evidence suggests a more coastal path along the so-called Kelp Highway. Back then a coast ran from Indonesia all the way north to Siberia, along the Bering Land Bridge and down the coast of North America to the bottom of South America. And this coast was a hotbed for wildlife thanks to its abundant namesake seaweed.

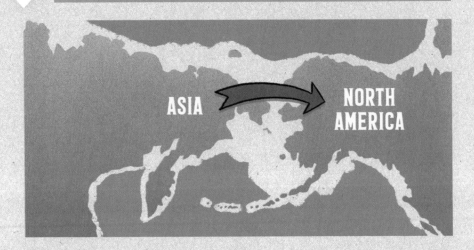

Before humans arrived in the Americas, journeys were mostly completed over land or short distances by water. Reaching the Americas from Asia was a task that we humans had to work up to over tens of thousands of years of wandering around, following the weather and whatever food we could get our hands on. As early nomadic (always traveling) groups stalked herds of large animals and made their way over continents, not only were we getting better at moving across large distances but our brains were actually adapting to navigation.

There are two major ways scientists believe our brains adapted to navigation over the hundreds of thousands of years of spreading around the planet: **cognitive mapping** and an **internal compass**. First, with cognitive mapping, we started to develop an understanding of a physical environment in our imagination. That means our brains were making maps in our heads way before anyone ever drew or conceived of them. This skill allowed us to do some very cool stuff as we moved through the world: Cognitive mapping helps us remember where we've been, create landmarks to reference as we move, and make route-making decisions.

Maps (even ones that only exist in our heads) aren't too useful if we don't have a sense of direction. Our ancestors' brains also developed the ability to sense direction and changes in direction. Wedged in the part of the brain responsible for memory, this internal compass is constantly recalibrating as we move throughout the world.

Our internal compass, however, isn't as nifty as our animal friends'. Ours works more like a heat-seeking missile—we decide on a goal and even if we get turned around a few times, we're still able to redirect toward that goal. Then as we move around, our brains can keep track of that direction. It's pretty basic—especially compared to the much better systems animals have—but it was good enough for the first navigators. Combined with cognitive mapping, this internal compass gave us *Homo sapiens* the ability to cross the vast deserts, plains, and waterways.

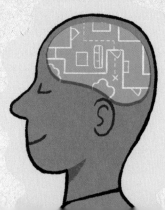

Animals
THE ORIGINAL NAVIGATORS

Ever wonder how animals know where they're going when they migrate? Like humans, animals use a mix of methods to find their way, like smell and sight. But some especially gifted animals have a navigational superpower: magnetite. This mineral is the most magnetic natural material on Earth, and it's found in certain animals' nervous systems, giving them a sort of built-in compass. Here are a few animals that utilize magnetite to read the earth's magnetic field:

LOGGERHEAD TURTLES: When it's time to mate and lay eggs, these ocean travelers return thousands of miles to the beach they hatched from. Everywhere on Earth has a unique magnetic signature, sort of like an address. By sensing the earth's magnetic field, loggerhead turtles return to the exact spot where they were born to find a partner and lay eggs of their own.

HOMING PIGEONS: The original mail carriers, these avian messengers have a knack for returning home even when they're released from unfamiliar areas. The phenomenon stumped scientists for centuries, but now we know they use a mix of an internal compass, their sense of smell, and the ability to follow low-frequency sounds that are undetectable to humans.

BLIND MOLE RATS: A species doesn't survive for thousands of years by luck alone. This blind, subterranean (underground) rodent has some hidden talents. Mole rats can both navigate using the earth's magnetic field and orient themselves if they get off track—all without other clues from the sun.

DOGS: Our canine friends navigate mostly with their sense of smell, but research shows they do have some ability to detect the earth's magnetic fields. How do they use it? One study shows that dogs off-leash tend to do their business (yup, #1 and #2) in alignment with north and south. Why? Scientists aren't sure, but it proves they are one more animal with an internal compass.

ACTIVITY

MAP IT OUT

Part 1:

Improving your cognitive mapping skills is a great first step toward becoming a globe-trotting navigator. With this quick exercise, you'll get a sense of how well you know your environment and the way you navigate it.

SUPPLIES NEEDED: blank paper, a pencil

1 Think of a place you know inside and out, like your house or school.

2 On a blank piece of paper, draw out the floor plan of the space.

3 Think especially about how you might move through the building and note any landmarks (like a favorite water fountain, the refrigerator, or your pet's bed) that might help you find your way.

Part 2:

Next choose a place you don't know so well. This could be a friend's house, a department store, or for a bigger challenge, the woods (be sure to bring a friend or grown-up).

 Walk through the new area once.

2 **Now grab a sheet of paper and do your best to draw a map from memory.**

3 **Trace the route you took and include as many landmarks as you can.**

4 **Now compare the two maps.**

Which is more detailed? Are they both accurate? What would you do differently to make your maps more useful?

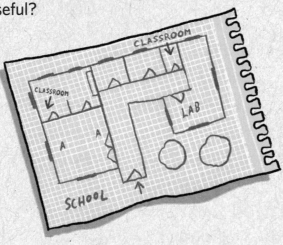

THE OLDEST POOP IN AMERICA (LITERALLY)

Tracing human migration requires evidence, and sometimes it's . . . a littly icky. Archaeologists found the continent's oldest human coprolite—that's fossilized poop—in Oregon dating back 14,300 years. The discovery is one of many pieces in the puzzle of how and when we arrived in the Americas.

THE BIG, BRIGHT, BURNING CALENDAR IN THE SKY

Early navigators relied on their entire environment to find their way. Let's start with the most glaringly obvious thing (yes, pun intended): the sun. Life on Earth would be impossible without the sun as it's our main source of energy. But the sun also has a job as our handy natural daytime compass and clock.

The sun can be a helpful guide if you want to know what time of day it is. No matter what, the sun always rises in the east and sets in the west. Whether you're in Antarctica, Atlanta, Australia, or Andalusia (that's in Spain), the sun will come up in the east in the morning, reach its highest point at noon, and finally go down in the west in the evening. Simple, right? Ancient humans may not have understood the reasons for the sun's movements, but they knew that tracking the sun's progress could help you know where you're going. Over time people gradually got better at getting around. We eventually turned navigation from an instinct to an art—and later to a science.

Possibly the first major breakthrough in tracking the movement of the sun dates back to around 7,000 years ago. Back then we were just getting the hang of planting food and agriculture. We were still a few thousand years away from the first known wheel, and technology was still really basic. That's why this astronomical invention called the **Goseck Circle** is so impressive. Located in present-day Germany, it looks like the world's easiest grass maze or maybe the world's largest bull's-eye. But its four rings acted as an accurate calendar to show the passage of years and seasons.

ROOTS OF THE WORDS

Across cultures around the world, the names for north, south, east, and west have their origin in where the sun rises and sets.

In English, the word *east* traces its roots to the early development of the German language. *Ostan* literally meant "toward the sun" in German. *North* originates from the Old German word *nord*, which may have come from an even older language called Proto-Indo-European (PIE). This ancient tongue gave birth to many languages

Gates were carefully placed around the circles, and when the sun lined up in a particular position with a gate, the viewer could determine the season.

in Europe and Asia. Here's where the directions and what we call them gets even more interesting.

Researchers believe *nord* comes from the PIE word *ner*, meaning "left"—as in when you're facing the rising sun in the east, north is to the left. *West* similarly relates to the sun, with roots from the PIE word *wes*, meaning "evening," when the sun sets. For the word *south*, it's all about the sun itself. The ancient PIE word for sun was *sawel*, which gave way to the Old English *sud*.

The Goseck Circle helped farmers prepare for each season by planning when to plant their crops. Earth calendars like the Goseck Circle appeared around Europe and parts of Central Asia and North America over the next few thousand years. People were beginning to understand time and direction by using the sun as a guide. From the Nabta Playa calendar in Egypt to Stonehenge in England to the great Majorville Medicine Wheel in Canada (which is larger than 100 American football fields), people around the world were building sites to track the movement of that burning ball in the sky that gives us life.

ACTIVITY

WHICH WAY? KNOW YOUR DIRECTIONS

Let's get familiar with the basics. No matter where you are on the earth, the order of north, east, south, and west is always the same. Because once you've found one of them, you can figure out the rest. Try a test run for fun.

1 Face whichever way you think is north (you might be wrong but that's okay for now as we're just getting started).

2 Hold your right arm out to the side and point. That's east.

3 Hold your left arm out to the side and point. That's west.

4 Directly in front and behind you? Yup, that's north and south.

These cardinal directions are the building blocks of most navigation techniques, so it's good to practice them and have them become second nature. And if you have trouble remembering them, go clockwise starting with north, to east, to south, to west. Or just remember this very important piece of life advice: **N**ever **E**at **S**oggy **W**affles.

CLUES IN THE TREES

Like us humans, all of nature is dependent on the sun. The way the sun moves through the sky affects the landscape and wildlife below. But no lifeforms are more sensitive to the sun than plants. Through a process called **photosynthesis**, plants convert the sun's energy into their own chemical energy. That chemical energy transforms water and carbon dioxide into oxygen (that we get to breathe) and organic compounds (like fruits and vegetables that we get to eat).

For thousands of years explorers and trackers around the world have used plants as a basic compass. Think of the plants in your house or classroom. Have you ever noticed how they tend to reach for the light? A plant hidden away in a bookshelf will reach its way toward a window as a survival mechanism.

Trees and plants in the wild behave the same way. Let's consider a tree in a forest: It's really no different from our photosynthetic friend in the bookshelf.

Tree branches will reach for wherever there's the most sunlight and even influence the growth of the tree. Have you ever seen a tree that's fully symmetrical? Probably not.

That's because trees have more or bigger branches on the side that gets more sun. In the Northern Hemisphere, that's the south side. Live below the **equator** (the imaginary line around the exact middle of the planet) in the Southern Hemisphere? Your trees will have more branches on the north side. This phenomenon of plants growing toward light is called **phototropism**. If the trees are telling you which way is north and which way is south, these clues can help you find your way.

The density of branches is just one clue trees offer. Look closely at the illustration below on the opposite page. There are more branches on the south side where the tree can get more sunlight. But what else is different about the two sides? Check out the direction the branches are growing in. On the north side (where there's less sun) the branches grow vertically, reaching straight up to get the most sun possible. Meanwhile, on the south side (where there are more rays to soak up) the branches grow outward and away from the trunk. This effect is most noticeable with deciduous trees—those are the type of trees that lose their leaves in the fall.

Of course, not every tree will behave this way and any navigator will tell you that you shouldn't base your bearings on just one. Think of some of the other factors that could influence a tree to grow. Strong **prevailing winds**, or winds that consistently blow in the same direction, can shape trees as much as the sun. On the windward side (where the wind hits) the branches might be scraggly and dense with fewer leaves. You'll find fuller branches on the sheltered, or leeward, side. In areas with extreme winds, you might find all the branches on this side!

FOLLOW THAT TREE!

In forests throughout North America, Native American tribes like the Cherokee, Ojibwe, and Potawatomi used to bend trees to create trails that covered hundreds of miles. Known as trail trees, these bent trees acted as landmarks to make navigating easier.

Creating a trail tree took time and patience. Navigators started by bending a young sapling in the direction they wanted it to point. Then they weighed it down with an animal hide and a rock. After a few years, they returned to untie the weight so the tree could then grow straight upward. Most trail trees have a distinct L shape, and because the bend started forming when the tree was young, the bend is usually close to the ground. Many of these trail trees still stand today—keep an eye out the next time you're hiking in the woods!

If you're exploring a dense evergreen forest where the branches appear the same, don't worry—nature still has clues for you. Instead of looking up at the branch patterns, get up close and personal with a few trees. Pay careful attention to the moss and lichens (plantlike organisms that sort of look like algae) on tree bark. In the Northern Hemisphere, moss generally grows on the north side of trees. That's because moss needs a damp, shady environment to thrive. The side of trees receiving *less* sunlight is usually the best spot for it to grow.

Other factors like steep terrain or consistent rain, however, can create damp shade where moss might thrive in any direction. The solution? Check lots of trees in an area. If there's one side that keeps showing up mossy, that's likely north. Even though every tree's growth will tell us something about directions, there might be other factors that we newbie navigators aren't quite wise to. That's why it's best to gather as many clues as possible—find a few trees of the same species that show the same signs to confirm our directions.

1. Visit a park with plenty of trees and open space during the day.

2. From a distance, locate a tree, then both you and your friend sketch it out, paying close attention to the branches.

3. Repeat this process a few times with different trees.

4. Now get up close and personal. Do you notice any moss or lichens on the bark?

5. Take note of other factors around you like wind and any birds or animals.

6. Keep this part to yourself! Beneath each sketch, write which direction you think the tree is facing.

7. Compare sketches and notes with your friend. Did you come up with the same directions?

8. Check to see if your directions were right using a local map or GPS.

9. What were some of the factors that influenced your decision? What plants or animals are unique to your area?

SPOT LIGHT

Directions in the Dunes

We're not always lucky enough to be surrounded by our leafy arboreal friends (ahem, trees) for navigation clues. But humans are remarkable when it comes to adapting to challenging environments—like massive expanses of desert. The Bedouin people of North Africa and the Arabian Peninsula have been reading the shapes of the sand dunes for thousands of years. This nomadic people traversed thousands of miles of blistering hot desert, where landmarks are scarce and tracks disappear in seconds. How'd they do it?

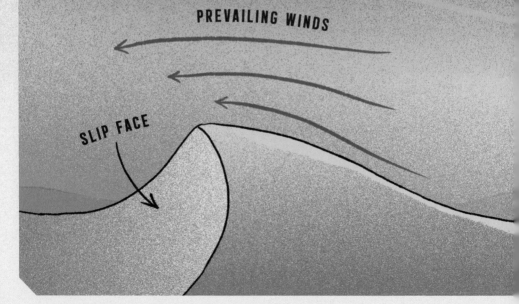

PREVAILING WINDS

SLIP FACE

In the winter months when sandstorms blew in clouds and the sun and stars weren't visible, Bedouins analyzed the sand. Large dunes form because of strong prevailing winds. If we know the prevailing winds in our desert come from the east, for instance, the dunes will form in a north-south direction with the less steep side facing the east and the steeper side, called the slip face, to the west.

Luckily this technique doesn't require a desert's worth of sand to see it in full effect. On a windy day, head to the beach or a park with a sandbox to inspect what kind of dunes form. Can you locate the windward side? Do you notice different properties in the sand's firmness on the slip face?

ANCIENT POLYNESIANS: FINDING CLUES IN THE OCEAN

When we find ourselves away from terra firma (dry land) altogether, nature has clues that can help us find our way in the middle of the ocean. Polynesian voyagers in the southern Pacific Ocean confidently sailed thousands of miles on the high seas long before the era of maps, compasses, and other navigational tools. They did it by carefully reading the movement of the sea beneath them and watching for birds overhead.

Although seabirds spend most of their time soaring in the sky, they do need to nest and lay eggs sometime. So depending on the time of year, migrating birds were one clue these sailors might follow to find land. According to Polynesian oral histories, sailors kept a special family of tropical seabirds called frigate birds as pets on board. Frigate birds hate getting wet, so when sailors needed a nudge in the right direction, they'd set the birds free, trusting they'd fly to the closest island.

It wasn't just following birds, however, that allowed these seafaring people to cross unprecedented distances of open ocean—it was their relationship with the water.

Spread out over thousands of islands, Polynesians have many distinct cultures. But one thing unites them: the sea. In fact, there's a common belief in Polynesia that the ocean doesn't separate islands but connects them.

By 300 CE, Polynesians had become some of the earliest and most successful navigators—who prefer the term **wayfinders**. If navigating is the precise science of getting around, wayfinding is the art of training your mind to memorize positioning and directional clues. Many outsiders would simply see the waters of the open ocean as chaotic, like a big hot tub with the jets on full blast, but Polynesians saw pathways.

Through constant observation and generations of elders teaching the next generation, Polynesians read the movements of the oceans to find their way across open water. Even so, there's some debate over exactly how the 10 million square miles (16,000,000 km²)—that's bigger than the United States, Canada, and Mexico combined!—of ocean were settled. Researchers believe the Polynesians descended from the Lapita people, who originally traveled by boat down from southern China around 3000 BCE. Over the next 1,500 years the Lapita spread throughout the Pacific.

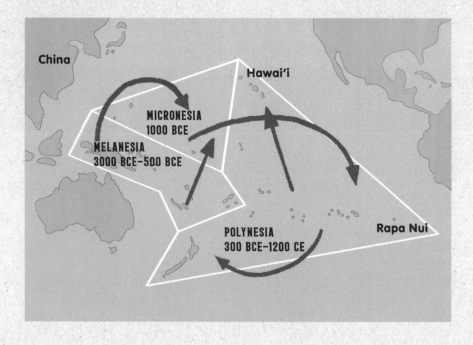

When they were island-hopping looking for new lands to settle, the Lapita initially skipped already populated Melanesia (today's Papua New Guinea, Solomon Islands, Fiji, and Vanuatu). It's part of the reason we know they were confident seafarers. Instead they kept pushing farther out into the ocean, reaching east to what we now know as Polynesia and north to Micronesia.

As the Lapita pushed out to these new lands, distinct cultures developed, and with them, new ways of navigating. DNA evidence shows that later on the Melanesians and Lapita-descended Polynesians mixed. But it was mainly male Melanesians traveling to Polynesia, likely on fishing expeditions.

The Polynesians would continue crossing larger distances of open ocean as their navigational abilities improved, reaching Tahiti around 700 CE, Hawai'i around 900 CE, and Rapa Nui (also known as Easter Island, the one full of epic stone statues) in 1200 CE. While just about every other sailor in the world (save for those fearless Vikings) still clung within sight of the shore, these early explorers were centuries ahead in their ability to move across open ocean. We know they sometimes followed birds, but they also used the position of the stars and the movement of the waves. So how did they do it?

Have you ever looked out to the ocean or a large lake and noticed the surface looks like corduroy with neat rows lined up? Those lines are called **swells** and they're caused by prevailing winds, which blow in the same direction consistently from far away. The Polynesians navigated using swells created by the **trade winds**, a type of prevailing wind.

Trade winds blow constantly from the east toward the west around the equator. These winds helped humans buy and sell goods. The name was coined in the 1600s, and *trade* is Middle English for "path." They're created by hot air moving up (heat always rises!) around the equator with colder air rushing in to take its place. And conveniently, this constant, steady movement helps us humans cross the oceans.

These nifty trade winds created reliable swell patterns that Polynesian navigators could rely on. In open ocean, swells move in straight lines. The Polynesians were so tuned in to how the ocean moved that they could determine their direction by the way their boats rocked. If a navigator knows from generations of observation that the trade winds in their area create a swell that moves from southeast to northwest, they can tell which direction they're heading in based on how their boat moves.

THE CANOES BUILT FOR CROSSING OCEANS

For journeys over open seas, Polynesians developed the outrigger canoe. While single-hull canoes are tippy and slow in rough water, this design features a support float (its namesake outrigger) that runs parallel to the main hull where the paddlers sit. The extra stability was necessary for crossing thousands of miles of rough water—and so was some serious paddle power. On long hauls, sails provided some extra push, but most of the power came from hard paddling. And don't expect any fancy sleeping quarters—early Polynesian vessels barely had enough room to sit, and there's a good chance everyone on board was soaked day and night.

Sailing Over Swells

H ere are the three main boat movements that ancient Polynesians would pay attention to when sailing over swells:

PITCHING: This is when the direction of the boat is moving either with or directly against the waves in the swell. It's called pitching because the front (bow) and back (stern) of the boat are hurled up and down as we cross the rolling waves.

In this example, the swell is coming from the west. If we're pitching, our boat (let's call it the SS *Knowitall*) would point either east or west. If we're facing east, it's moving with the swell, so the stern of the boat will rise up first. If we travel west, we're moving against the swell, and the bow of the boat will rise up first.

ROLLING: This is the opposite of pitching, and seasick sailors should start to get worried. Now we're traveling along the lines of the swell, so as each wave in the swell passes us, the SS *Knowitall* will roll. The side of the boat that begins to roll first can tell us about which direction we're headed.

If we're rolling, we're sailing either north or south. Picture yourself on the SS *Knowitall* and the right side (starboard) begins the roll as the wave passes under the boat. Based on what we know about our swell direction, if the starboard side starts the roll that means we're heading north. Let's take a U-turn. Now we're sailing south, which means the left side (port) will start rolling first.

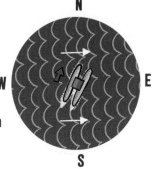

CORKSCREWING: This is where the seasickness can really set in. Corkscrewing is when the boat pitches and rolls at the same time. This happens when we travel diagonally to the swell. That means the SS *Knowitall* would be traveling either due northwest, northeast, southeast, or southwest. Based on what we know about pitching and rolling, can you determine how the SS *Knowitall* would move for each direction?

Southeast: Pitching stern, rolling port. Southwest: Pitching bow, rolling port.

Northeast: Pitching stern, rolling starboard. Northwest: Pitching bow, rolling starboard.

MAPPING THE MOODS OF THE SEA

Going back to around 1500 BCE, master navigators held high positions in ancient Polynesian society. A group of elders selected promising young students to take on the training as children. Their training could last decades, and each new navigator was expected to pass their wisdom on to the next generation.

Even seasoned professionals needed to brush up on their knowledge. There are over 1,000 islands in Polynesia (a number that is constantly changing as new islands form and others get washed over), so navigators needed to develop some kind of record of how swells behaved in their neck of the ocean. The result is a type of mapmaking that's unique to this part of the world and a map that's only readable to the person who made it.

Stick charts (also called rebbelibs, medos, and mattangs) were crafted in various cultures around Polynesia. These maps reflect the movements of swells relative to islands and reefs. Many land-based people often think of the ocean on maps as empty spaces, but wayfinders know it's where all the activity and key information is found. Wayfinders used pieces of palm tree fronds and sticks to show the bend of swells, and pebbles or shells represented islands. Straight sticks generally depicted underlying currents, and the closer they were together, the stronger the current.

Every wayfinder made their own stick chart depending on the waters they wanted to cross. The chart only served the wayfinder who made it, and they didn't even bring it with them on the boat! They memorized the patterns on their chart and navigated off the feel of the ocean. The charts were heavily guarded, as was the knowledge of how to make and use them. One thing never changes: Knowledge is power.

Navigating using clues from the natural world is just part of the puzzle. Navigators throughout history have used multiple sources of information from the environment around them at the same time. Paying attention to nature and piecing together some of these clues helps us build up our observational skills, but it's only the beginning!

MAKE YOUR OWN STICK CHART

SUPPLIES NEEDED: Get creative here. You can use sticks, straws, string, pebbles, or whatever is around you. Floss comes in handy for binding your materials together!

1. Find a body of water to chart—it can be as big as the ocean or as small as a puddle. Start by carefully observing the area.

2. Pay close attention to how any breezes move the water, and note any changes in the pattern of ripples.

3. Note any landmarks that could be used as a reference in your map. These could be an island offshore or a rock in the middle of a puddle.

Let's get charted! Start by using your materials to build a frame for your chart.

⑤ Next use bendable materials like chenille stems (also called pipe cleaners) or aluminum wire to illustrate the surface of the water. Was it really chopping when the wind blew from a certain direction? Place your materials closer together to show a stronger force.

⑥ Is there a landmark that might help you orient? Include it in your map using a pebble (or whatever will best remind you of that marker).

⑦ When you're finished, see if you can memorize some of the patterns you've created.

⑧ Show a friend the finished product, and enjoy the confused look on their face when you tell them it's an ancient system for mapping the ocean and you're the only one who can read this one!

-2-

NATURE'S MAP IN THE SKY

THE SUN AND STARS

Every day the world around us changes in countless ways. It's been this way for the last four and a half giga-annums—that's 4.5 billion years, about how long the earth has been around. There are big, slow changes, like the movement of continents (thanks, plate tectonics). Then there are the sorts of changes we can see right in front of us, from buildings being constructed to islands emerging in the middle of the sea. With the earth in a constant state of change, navigating with certainty requires a permanent guide: the sun and stars.

Successful navigation requires using all of the tools and clues made available to us. In Chapter 1, we learned how to determine direction using the sun and nature as a guide. Now we'll take our navigation skills to the next level using nature's map in the sky. Just like our planet, the sun and stars are also in a constant state of change. But luckily that change comes slowly—on the scale of millions to billions of years—so we can count on their predictable patterns to help us get around.

Thanks to our wild imaginations and unyielding quest to make sense of the world, it didn't take long for societies all around the planet to start using the stars as tools.

The first known written account of celestial navigation is in Homer's epic poem the *Odyssey*, composed sometime around 800 BCE. The hero, Odysseus, and his shipmates use the stars as aids on the long journey to stay on course through the sea. The ancient Greeks were early adopters of astronomy, but they weren't the first. Even if early cultures didn't fully understand the science around star navigation, many of them became experts thousands of years ago.

FOLLOWING THE STARS ACROSS THE OCEAN

One of the earliest societies to master celestial wayfinding at sea was the ancient Polynesians around 3000 CE. Remember how they used clues from the sea and nature around them to travel across thousands of miles of open ocean? They did it by taking notice of all of their surroundings, including the stars overhead. In fact, with little in the way of landmarks, the stars were one of the few constant sights they could count on.

Life as a Polynesian wayfinder on a long journey meant hard work with barely any sleep. While keeping an eye on the pattern of the waves, wind, and any wildlife, the wayfinder also read the stars above and only took catnaps. Similar to how they used stick charts, wayfinders memorized hundreds of star positions and names prior to setting out on a journey. They were taught by older wayfinders and shared the tradition through storytelling. On their open-voyaging canoes—made of two long, hollowed out tree trunks with a deck across the top—these wayfinders couldn't risk losing a map to the stars, so they memorized them.

Though this knowledge helped make them such experts at celestial navigation, the tradition was nearly lost after centuries of European colonial rule. Fortunately, Nainoa Thompson and other Pwo (that means "master" in the Micronesian tradition) wayfinders from the Polynesian Voyaging Society in Hawai'i have kept these techniques alive today.

NAVIGATING WITH THE STAR WE KNOW BEST: THE SUN

Ready to navigate with the stars? Let's start with the one we're most familiar with on a daily basis: the sun. While the sun literally gives us life, it also acts as our clock in the sky. The very concept of time is built on the earth's rotation (spinning at a blistering 1,000 miles or 1,609km per hour) and the rising and setting of the sun throughout the day and the year. The sun rises in the east and sets in the west.

Ancient societies around the world caught on to this movement and used it to help them find their directions. As early as 3500 BCE, humans were measuring the sun's movements using a simple pillar in the ground called a **gnomon**. A few thousand years later in 1300 BCE, the Egyptians developed the shadow clock, or **sundial**, that laid the foundation for clocks as we know them today. Now let's make our own version.

GET YOUR BEARINGS USING THE SUN

The stars might get all the shine when it comes to finding your cardinal directions, but during the day the sun is the only available option. There are several ways to use the sun to find north, south, east, and west, but here are the two easy methods.

Part 1:
The Shadow Method

SUPPLIES NEEDED: a wide-open patch of grass, four pieces of scrap paper, two sticks, a marker, and two rocks.

1 **For beginners, do this on a clear, sunny day in the morning or midafternoon.**

2 **In your open patch of grass where the sun is shining, place your stick in the ground so it's sticking upright. It's best to find one that's straight and at least 3 feet (about a meter) long. If you've got one, use a yardstick or meterstick.**

3 Note the shadow the stick makes and mark the end of the shadow by placing a rock there.

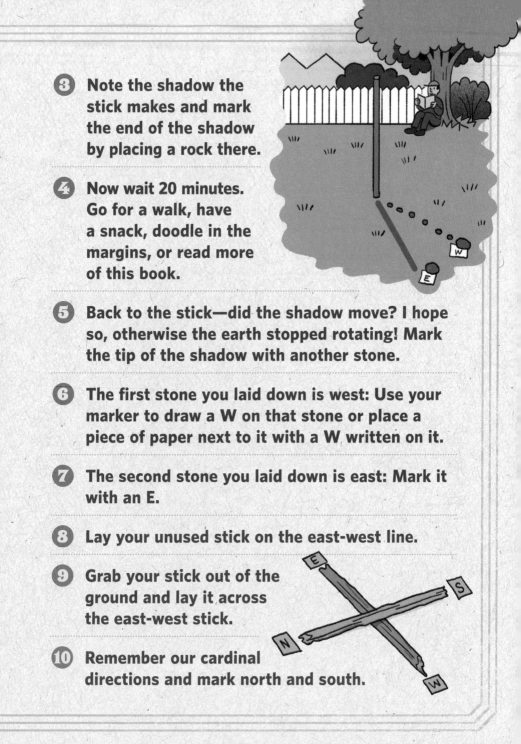

4 Now wait 20 minutes. Go for a walk, have a snack, doodle in the margins, or read more of this book.

5 Back to the stick—did the shadow move? I hope so, otherwise the earth stopped rotating! Mark the tip of the shadow with another stone.

6 The first stone you laid down is west: Use your marker to draw a **W** on that stone or place a piece of paper next to it with a **W** written on it.

7 The second stone you laid down is east: Mark it with an **E**.

8 Lay your unused stick on the east-west line.

9 Grab your stick out of the ground and lay it across the east-west stick.

10 Remember our cardinal directions and mark north and south.

Part 2:
The Clock Face Method

For navigators in a hurry, there's another method to use the sun to find cardinal directions. Try this one on a sunny day in midmorning or midafternoon in a place without many obstructions, like an open field or park.

> **SUPPLIES NEEDED:** either an analog watch (the old-school kind with a minute and hour hand) or some sort of device to tell time (it could be a digital watch or phone), a marker, and paper.

1 If you have an analog watch, make sure the time is correct.

2 If you don't have an analog watch, use a marker to draw out a clock face on the paper for the current time as it reads on your watch or phone.

3 With your watch or clock face drawing lying flat in your palm, point the hour hand (that's the shorter one!) toward the sun.

4 Notice the angle between the hour hand pointing at the sun and 12 o'clock on your watch face.

5 Find the midpoint of the angle and draw or imagine a line through it, going away from you. That is south.

6 Extend that same line through the middle of your clock face in the other direction—that's north.

7 With your north-south line all set, draw or imagine a line across it for east-west.

READING THE POLESTARS: OUR WAY TO NORTH AND SOUTH

If you've ever found yourself outside on a clear night and looked overhead, the sheer number of stars is staggering. On the best nights, the naked eye can spot about 4,500 stars from anywhere on the planet. Since we can only be in one hemisphere at a time, we see just half the stars visible from Earth. That means if you took a trip across the equator to the opposite hemisphere, you'd see a different 4,500 stars! With all those stars it's easy to get overwhelmed, but with a little know-how, the night sky will provide a wealth of information. First, let's look at how our relationship to stars from here on the earth works.

As we've mentioned, we live on a rotating planet. But the stars, including the sun, remain in fixed positions. That means depending on where we are on Earth, we see different stars rise and set at different angles. Lucky for us, there are special stars called **polestars** that we can use as anchor points in both the Northern Hemisphere and Southern Hemisphere to help us find our way.

The North Star, also known as Polaris, is your best friend when navigating in the Northern Hemisphere (where 90 percent of people live). The **constellation** (group of stars) known as the Crux is your guide for the Southern Hemisphere. Polaris gets its distinction as the North Star because it lies approximately in a straight line off the North Pole. The same goes for the Crux, which lies straight off the South Pole.

POLESTAR PRIDE

The Crux inspires some serious pride in the Southern Hemisphere. So much so that it appears on five national flags for countries below the equator: Australia, Brazil, New Zealand, Papua New Guinea, and Samoa.

AUSTRALIA

BRAZIL

NEW ZEALAND

PAPUA NEW GUINEA

SAMOA

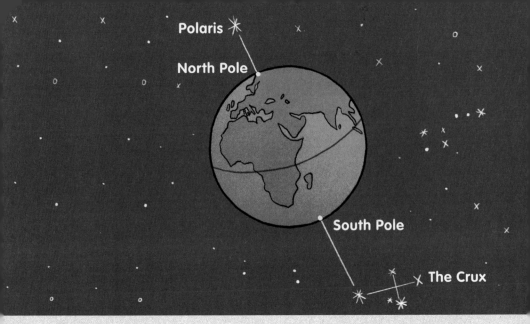

Polaris and the Crux act as our guides to help us find north or south. If you're in the Northern Hemisphere and looking at Polaris, that's north. Walk in the direction of Polaris and you'll always be walking north until you hit

LIGHT CHECK

When it comes to navigation, it's no wonder we hear so much about these polestars. But if the earth is rotating all the time and the stars are rising and setting, why does Polaris always indicate north? Here's one way to understand—just try not to get dizzy:

Look up at the ceiling and choose a point directly overhead, like a light fixture. That will serve as your the North Pole—in which case remember to bring a jacket. The same goes for the Crux in the Southern Hemisphere. If you're south of the equator and locate the Crux, that direction is always south. Keep following the Crux and you'll eventually hit the South Pole—also bring a jacket and a few spare fish snacks to share because that's the pole with penguins!

Polaris and the Crux are handy and reliable navigational tools, but in astronomical terms they won't stay the same forever. Because the earth rotates on a tilt, there's an effect called **precession**. It's a lot like what happens when you spin a top and it starts wobbling—but it's the entire earth wobbling, and one full wobble takes about 26,000 years.

polestar. Now spin around in circles directly under the polestar with your gaze fixed on that marker. What do you notice? The marker you're under doesn't move even as you spin. Check out other points on the ceiling around your polestar. Notice how they make a perfect circular pattern? This is just like how the stars rise and set around Polaris and the Crux, but those navigational stars themselves don't appear to move as the earth rotates.

As the wobble continues (or "axial precession," if we're really putting on our lab coats), the direction the poles are facing changes and so do the stars that line up with the North and South Poles. When pyramids sprang up in Egypt around 2630 BCE, a star called Thuban was the Northern Hemisphere's polestar of its day. In 13,000 years, we'll have the superbright star called Vega showing us the way north. (Don't hold your breath waiting!)

We're currently wobbling toward Polaris lining up perfectly with the celestial North Pole, so it will continue to become even more accurate. Mark your calendars, because on March 24, 2100, Polaris will be as closely lined up with the celestial North Pole as it will ever get. Any idea of what the North Star will be in 26,000 years? That's right, we'll have Polaris guiding the way north again.

Thuban

FINDING POLARIS

Polaris is in the constellation Ursa Minor, which is Latin for "Little Bear." Ursa Minor is now widely known in North America as the Little Dipper (yes, it's the one that looks like a tiny spoon), but people have given it many names throughout history.

Ancient societies often told complex stories relating to the figures they saw in the constellations. Some societies like the ancient Greeks used the constellations to tell of the gods and mythical creatures they believed created the earth. Every society's reading of the stars was different, but they all saw the same stars (depending on the hemisphere, of course) and noticed some of the same major patterns. Now we'll look at how to find the North Star.

A Map to the North Star

No matter what you call it, finding Ursa Minor is easiest if you start by locating its bigger buddy, Ursa Major, also known as the Big Dipper.

Since we're looking for the North Star (Polaris) and the Big Dipper points us in that direction, we can assume the Big Dipper is somewhere in the northern section of the sky. Use what you know about where the sun sets (in the west) to find the northern part of the sky. Once you've found the Big Dipper, locate the two stars that make up the outer wall of the ladle (named Dubhe and Merak). If the Big Dipper were a spoon, this is the first part that hits the milk and cereal when you're eating breakfast.

Now trace an imaginary line from those two stars heading in the direction away from the open part of the ladle. Following that line will bring you to Ursa Minor and more specifically, right to Polaris. It's a distance of about five times the edge of the Big Dipper (the distance between Dubhe and Merak). Polaris is the tail of the Little Bear or the very end of the spoon handle. Now you're facing north.

Ursa Minor

Polaris

Ursa Major

Dubhe

Merak

ACTIVITY

MAKE YOUR OWN STAR CLOCK

Let's take our skills to the next level. Time and navigation are linked in several ways that we'll dive deep into in Chapter 3, but here are the two main reasons how: Time helps us determine how far you've traveled and your position east or west from a known point. Using the stars to tell time seems like an impossible superpower at first, but with a little know-how, a star clock, and some math, it's as easy as looking up.

SUPPLIES NEEDED: a clear starry night, a paper plate, and a pen.

1. **Mark the paper plate with hour markers, but don't just copy a normal 12-hour clock. For this star clock, we'll have 24 hours, and the numbers will run counterclockwise. Start at the top, where you'd normally find 12 o'clock and mark it 0. Make your way around the clock moving counterclockwise, marking 1 to 23, making sure the numbers are evenly spaced.**

2. **Mark the center of your clock as Polaris.**

3 Locate the Big Dipper and Polaris in the night sky.

4 Holding up your clock out in front of you as you look at Polaris, trace a line from Polaris past the tip of Ursa Major's ladle (Dubhe). The number that line crosses on our clock is the time.

5 Every year on March 6, this reading will tell you the time. Every other day of the year, you'll need to do some math.

6 Count the number of months since March 6 and multiply that number by two. Then subtract the result from the star time (from Step 4).

For instance, say it's May 20 (2.5 months after March 6). You measured a star time of 23:00. That's 2.5 × 2 = 5. Then, 23 – 5 = 18, or 6:00 p.m.

7 Add one hour for Daylight Saving Time if it's happening where you are. (For example, if you get an answer of 9:00 p.m. on July 13, it's actually 10:00 p.m. because of Daylight Saving Time.)

8 Check your results against a watch. How did you do?

ORION'S SIGNALS

Orion's belt is one of the most recognizable constellations in the Northern Hemisphere—it's also pretty useful. If the belt is vertical, that marks east. Use your thumb, index finger, and middle finger to make an E, with each finger representing a star. When the belt is horizontal, that marks west—and conveniently makes a W with your fingers!

THE CRUX: THE POLAR CONSTELLATION DOWN UNDER

In the Southern Hemisphere, instead of a single polestar there's a tiny constellation to guide navigators south. The Crux—Latin for "cross"—is often called the Southern Cross, and it resembles a kite. This five-star constellation is the smallest of all 88 recognized modern constellations. Luckily, there are two bright **pointer stars**. Those are stars that navigators rely on to locate constellations. The pointer stars Alpha Centauri and Beta Centauri help the Crux stand out in the night sky.

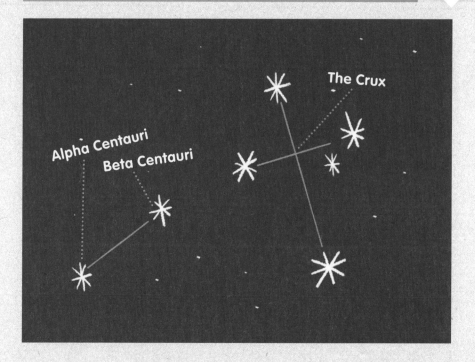

Unlike Polaris, the Crux isn't totally lined up with the celestial South Pole. Throughout the night, the Crux rotates slightly, just as Ursa Major does, so finding south will take an extra step. Start out by locating the Crux. Look in the general direction of south, which you'll know based on how the sun sets in the west. Then, most navigators look for the two bright pointer stars. These stars appear to point toward the top of the Crux. Notice the distance between the two pointer stars. The Crux is about two lengths of the pointer stars away.

Once you've found the Crux, imagine lines connecting the four stars to make a cross or kite (the fifth star is for style points). Here's an easy way to use it to find south: Draw an imaginary line from the top of the kite to the tail or from the top of the cross to the bottom. Extend that line out four times the length of the Crux. That point is south.

South Pole

FINDING LATITUDE WITH THE STARS

Polaris and the Crux are our surefire compasses in the sky for pointing us north and south, but that's not all we can learn from them. They also tell us how far north or south we are from the equator. That helps a navigator find their position and get to the next one.

You've already got everything you need to get a rough idea of your latitude. **Latitude** is the number we use to locate our north-south position on the earth. Meanwhile, **longitude** is for our east-west position. Navigators use imaginary lines called parallels to show their latitude. They're stacked from the equator all the way up (north) or down (south) to the poles. Parallels of latitude are written as degrees, but not the kind that tell the temperature. The equator is zero degrees latitude (0°) while the North Pole is 90 degrees north (90°N) and the South Pole is 90 degrees south (90°S).

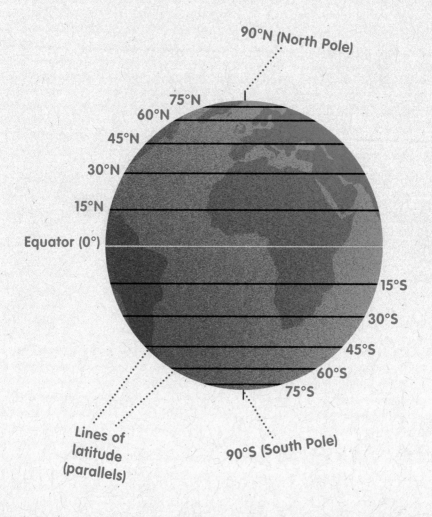

As we move farther north, Polaris rises increasingly high from the horizon. At the North Pole, or 90th parallel north, Polaris will shine almost directly overhead.

Meanwhile, moving south, Polaris sinks lower toward the horizon. By the time you hit the equator, Polaris is just on the horizon line at 0 degrees. The Crux in the Southern Hemisphere works the same way. As you travel south from the equator, the Crux moves higher in the sky. At the South Pole, or 90th parallel south, the Crux will be almost directly overhead.

WATCH OUT FOR COUNTERFEITS!

The False Cross is an imposter grouping of stars near the Crux that has led many navigators astray. Don't be fooled! Here's how to spot the fake:

1. It's not as bright.
2. It's missing those two spotlight pointer stars.
3. It's shaped like a plus sign instead of a kite.
4. It's missing the fifth star located outside the cross.
5. It won't point you south!

Now we'll learn the fist-stacking method to get a rough reading of our latitude. With a little extra work, we can then make a basic **sextant** that will give us a much more accurate reading. Sextants are tools used to measure the angle between the horizon and celestial objects. They first caught on for navigation in the early 1700s.

Early sextants were made of heavy and expensive materials like ivory and mahogany wood. There are simple ones (like the one we're making) and ornate brass sextants with double mirrors, telescopes, and sun shades. We'll start with an easy version using a few basic objects.

The Fist-Stacking Method

When we determine north or south using Polaris and the Crux, the angle from which we see the star also tells us how far we are from the pole. That way we can figure out our latitude. This works best in a wide-open area with a clear look at the horizon.

Start out by locating Polaris (or the Crux if you're in the Southern Hemisphere) on a clear night. Once you've found Polaris, hold one fist out all the way in front of you. Hold it out under Polaris so the bottom of your fist lines up with the horizon. Stack your other fist on top and repeat until

you reach Polaris. Each stacked fist counts as 10 degrees of latitude. If you hit Polaris somewhere mid-fist, estimate how high up your fist it reaches. The total number of stacked fists multiplied by 10 degrees equals the degree of latitude you are on. For example, four and a half fists stacked up would put you around 45 degrees north— exactly half way between the equator and the North Pole.

This skill works the same for everyone, big or small. Whether you're Sun Mingming (the tallest basketball player in the world, measuring in at 7'9", or 2.4m) or Tyrone "Muggsy" Bogues (the shortest player in NBA history at 5'3", or 1.6m), the results are the same. Try testing this out with someone bigger than you and someone smaller than you.

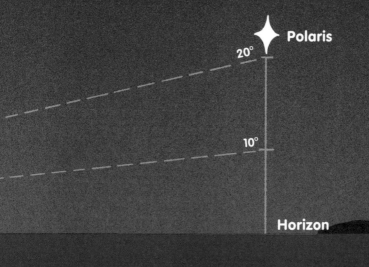

MAKE YOUR OWN BASIC SEXTANT

Let's measure your latitude with your very own sextant.

> **SUPPLIES NEEDED:** a small weight (like a washer), about 10 inches (25cm) of string, a 180-degree protractor (the D-shaped kind you might use in math class), a ruler that's at least 12 inches (30.5cm) long, masking tape, a clear starry night, a notebook to write down your results, and a friend.

1 Tie your weight to one end of your string.

2 Tie the string through the little hole in the protractor near the straight edge. (Most protractors have a hole here, but if yours doesn't, tape the string to the middle of the straight edge lined up with 90 degrees.)

3 Our rudimentary sextant is coming together. Tape the protractor to within an inch (2.5cm) of the end of your ruler. Line up the top edge of the ruler with the top edge of the straight side of your protractor. This will be your sight line.

4 Make sure the 180-degree mark of the protractor is facing the short end of your ruler and that your string can move freely. The 0-degree mark should be facing the longer end of your ruler. You'll be looking from this direction.

5 Now we're ready to take some readings. Let's try Polaris (or the Crux if you're below the equator). Hold the ruler so the sight-line edge is close to your eye—it helps to rest it on your cheekbone.

6 Line up the sight-line edge of the sextant with the polestar.

7 Stay steady! Have your friend note the number on the protractor that the string falls over. It should be between 0 and 90 degrees.

8 To calculate your latitude, subtract the value of your sighting from 90 degrees.

Let's say we measure Polaris at 51 degrees. 90 – 51 = 39. We're at 39 degrees north latitude, which runs through Washington, D.C., Kansas City, Beijing, and Lisbon, just to name a few places.

9 Compare the fist-stacking method to using your sextant—did you get a close answer? Was the sextant more accurate?

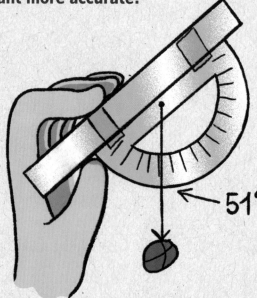

51°

TOOLS OF THE TRADE: MEASURING THE HEAVENS

Throughout history, cultures have crafted different devices to help determine their latitude. Among the earliest recorded is the **astrolabe**, first created by the Greeks in 200 BCE. These Frisbee-shaped devices tell time and the angle of the sun and stars. Sort of like a simple sextant, astrolabes are useful but bulky. Over the next 500 years, astrolabes became common throughout ancient Greece and later the Roman empire. Eventually the device spread east through the Islamic world, where astronomers continued to refine the astrolabe.

Around 700 CE, philosopher and astronomer Muhammad al-Fazari developed an astrolabe that helped measure time accurately. It gave an easier reading of the angle of rising and setting stars and even pointed worshippers in the direction of Mecca, the holiest city in Islam.

THE FIRST "COMPUTER" EVER

In 1900 a group of divers came across a Roman shipwreck full of treasures. Amid the vases and jewelry was a rusted-out collection of broken gears in a battered wooden frame. It's now referred to as the Antikythera mechanism, and it still has archaeologists scratching their heads in disbelief.

This mystery computer was about 1,000 years ahead of its time. Researchers have dated the device back to around 100 BCE. It wasn't until 2006 that they finally

Muslims face the direction of Mecca every time they pray, no matter where they are in the world. As Islamic astronomers improved their understanding of how our planet fit into the universe, so did their tools. Building on existing gadgets, they developed a series of tools called **quadrants** that could not only accurately measure the angle of celestial bodies but could also be carried easily.

started to understand how the mechanism worked. Scientists now believe it was used to track planetary movements and predict celestial events like eclipses. The mechanism was also used as a high-tech calendar and even kept track of the four-year cycle used for the ancient Olympics.

One of the simplest but most influential navigational instruments to come out of the Islamic world during this period was the **kamal**. Arab sailors created this effective tool around the 9th century. Its use spread quickly throughout Asia for **latitude sailing**—a method in which sailors first determine how far north or south their desired port is, sail to that latitude, and then sail east or west. It's safe to say this isn't the speediest route, but before you could punch in your destination on a map app, this was the most effective way!

The kamal is essentially a small rectangular piece of wood, about two inches by an inch (5cm x 2.5cm), with

Viking Navigation:
MYTH OR HISTORY?

Did you know Vikings were the first Europeans to sail to North America? They cruised over to what's now Newfoundland, Canada, about 500 years before Christopher Columbus set off on his famous journey to the New World in 1492. But was it all just by chance? Some researchers think so.

The Vikings were capable sailors, but archaeologists haven't found definitive proof of navigational tools. Viking sagas (stories passed down over generations) tell of crystals used to locate the sun when clouds and storms blew in. These so-called sólarsteins (sunstones) were likely hunks of the mineral calcite. In skilled hands they could be used to find the sun in even the cloudiest weather. Archaeologists are still on the lookout at dig sites for proof of sólarsteins, so this myth could one day become history.

a string coming out of the center. Knots are tied at regular intervals in the string, about a finger width apart. These are called the **isba** and they translate to about 1.5 degrees of latitude each.

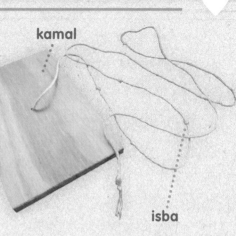

Navigators would hold the kamal out at arm's length with one end of the string in their mouth held taut. They lined up the bottom of the wood block with the horizon and the top edge with Polaris. Then, navigators counted the number of isba to add up their latitude.

It's suspected that the kamal influenced the design of the **cross-staff** (also known as the Jacob's staff) developed by French mathematician Levi ben Gerson in the 14th century. This device was more like a yardstick, equipped with degree markers and a sliding cross-section that the navigator lined up with whatever star they were measuring. Using a cross-staff looks a little like playing a trombone to the heavens.

TOOLS OF THE AGE OF EUROPEAN EXPLORATION

As the Middle Ages began to wind down around 1400, explorers started modifying older, more complicated devices to read the skies. Astrolabes were getting too heavy to bring on ships and difficult to use when the waters were anything but flat as a frozen pond. Sailors sought to create a slightly more portable version suited to life at sea, but there was a lot of work to do.

To remain steady in heavy breezes, astrolabes were made of heavy brass and so were cumbersome for sailors. Imagine holding a big, round weight (like a Frisbee made of iron) while you try to line up the horizon and Polaris on a rocking ship. Not easy. Sailors wanted more user-friendly tools, but it was also economics powering the innovation of navigation methods.

Beginning in the 1400s, the pursuit of land and power became more and more competitive in Europe, giving way to the Age of European Exploration and a time of great suffering for the rest of the world. For the next 400 years, European explorers exploited the resources and people of Asia and the Americas, and forcibly enslaved an estimated 15 million men, women, and children from Africa. For European countries, having their explorers sail reliably across oceans meant more access to lands to colonize and people to enslave. As a result, more dependable navigational tools were soon developed to make these long journeys.

Explorers from Portugal, the maritime superpower at the time, were the first to sail south of the equator in order to reach the west coast of Africa. They sailed without the aid of Polaris—meaning they needed to develop an instrument that could take a reading on the sun to determine latitude.

They created a highly effective and influential device called a **mariner's astrolabe**. It combined the portability of the quadrant developed by Islamic navigators with the accuracy of astrolabes used on land. The mariner's astrolabe allowed sailors to check their latitude even with Polaris nowhere to be found. Now they could measure the angle between another star or the sun and the horizon, called "taking a sight." Thanks to the tool's smaller size, they could even take readings on the rolling deck of a ship.

Navigators in this era were constant tinkerers and weren't afraid to borrow from other people's ideas. But reading north-south position was only half the puzzle of navigating. What about east-west? Explorers were completing full circle trips around the world, or **circumnavigating** the entire globe for at least 300 years before they created a system for figuring out their east-west position, or longitude. In the meantime, they carefully measured distance using methods we'll explore in the next chapter.

Using the sun and stars to navigate is a building block for knowing how to get around. The predictable pattern of the stars and the sun make them reliable tools for navigating. As we saw in this chapter, humans are drawn to figuring out how the world around them works and there are many ways of interpreting the sky above. The tools and techniques people developed through the centuries were informed by their location and their need to navigate. As we improved navigation skills, cultures were able to share ideas and push technology and knowledge forward.

-3-
DISTANCE AND DEAD RECKONING
A NEW ERA OF NAVIGATION

It might sound like an action-packed video game, but **dead reckoning** is actually one of the most important types of navigation. While we tend to focus mainly on the direction we're heading while finding our way, measuring distance is just as important. Dead reckoning is the process of figuring where you are based on two things: a known previous position (called the fix in navigation lingo, like a port or other landmark) along with the distance you've traveled on a given straight course.

In the last chapter we learned how to determine our latitude—the position north or south of the equator.

Long before navigators developed a system of finding east-west position with lines of longitude, they were using dead reckoning. This technique was a Band-Aid of sorts until the longitude problem could be solved. An English clockmaker cracked the case—learn all about it in Chapter 4.

HOW'D IT GET THAT NAME?

The origins of dead reckoning's undoubtedly cool name are murky. "Reckoning" refers to the quality of the measurement, meaning that it's a best guess based on the information you have. The "dead" part is a bit more unclear. Some historians argue the word "dead" should really be spelled "ded"—a shortened version of deduced reckoning, meaning it's a sort of logical conclusion. Others say "dead" simply refers to the direction you've got to keep moving for the system to work: dead ahead. It could also be an old sailor's phrase referencing the seriousness of getting it right—something to the tune of "if you don't reckon right, you'll be dead!"

THE EARLY DAYS OF DEAD RECKONING AT SEA

Christopher Columbus and the ocean-crossing seafarers of his day managed to travel far with minimal technology. They used the celestial navigation tools we looked at in Chapter 2 (to determine their north-south latitude) combined with basic compasses. The big issue, however, was calculating distance with dead reckoning. To do that, they had to measure how fast they traveled (speed) and how long it took them (time).

The clocks in that era couldn't keep time on a rolling ship, so sailors measured time with a **sandglass**. This simple device features two glass chambers connected by a narrow passage with a fine sand-like material inside. When all of the material falls from the top chamber to the bottom, the user knows a specific amount of time has passed.

Keeping time with a sandglass was easy but tedious. Measuring speed was a whole other story—the fact that sailors crossed oceans using these methods shows the power of basic math. When the captain needed a speed reading, a sailor would drop a piece of wood—called a **heave log**—off the bow (front) of the ship. A crew at the stern (back) of the boat called out when the heave log passed them. Crews knew the length of their ships, so that length multiplied by the time it took the heave log to pass gave them a speed.

Historians estimate that, when everything went well, this method worked out to about 90 percent accuracy. But a lot could mess with the old "throw a log off the ship and watch the sandglass" routine. Rough seas, currents, and wind all affected the speed of both the heave log and the ship. Not only could these factors make the heave log less reliable, but every time sailors noticed a major change in the speed or direction of the wind and currents, they had to start the dead reckoning process over and recalculate everything. Navigation crews on these ships were kept plenty busy by Mother Nature.

SPOT LIGHT Dead Reckoning Basics

Dead reckoning is all about measuring your distance from a known point to find out where you are. If you know where you started from and keep track of your speed, time, and direction, you'll have a good idea of where you ended up.

How do we do that? Use this handy formula to figure out distance: Distance = Speed × Time. Let's say you're at school and want to figure out how far you are from home. That's the distance. You know your school is due west of your house (the fix). Thanks to your trusty pair of sneakers, you're cruising at 3 miles per hour (4.8km/h), the average human walking speed, when you go to school. That's the speed. You time how long it takes you to get there and you clock in at exactly 30 minutes, or ½ hour. That's the time. So how far is your school from your house? Let's figure it out with dead reckoning.

We multiply our speed (3 miles per hour) by time (½ hour) to get the distance. Here's what it all looks like:

$$3 \text{ MILES PER HOUR} \times \tfrac{1}{2} \text{ HOUR} = 1.5 \text{ MILES (2.4KM)}$$
$$\text{(SPEED)} \times \text{(TIME)} = \text{(DISTANCE)}$$

Your house is 1.5 miles from school!

When using this formula for dead reckoning, it's critical that your direction remains exactly the same every time you calculate your distance. That means you should always be traveling in a straight line. If you need to change direction, you've got to start all over: Establish your fix and calculate distance again.

For example, let's say we want to figure out how far we're traveling when walking in the woods, where there are often lots of obstacles in the way and the trail curves around. The same applies if the terrain changes (like steeper, slower hiking) and there's a need to adjust your speed.

MEASURING SPEED, SLOWLY AND NOT ALWAYS SURELY

Sailors constantly kept an eye on their compasses and checked their speed every half hour. In order for dead reckoning to work, however, they needed to travel in a straight course. Sailors used basic compasses to stay on track to make their measurements without curving or zigzagging.

Sailors also had charts and tools called **traverse boards** to track their progress. Made of wood, pegs, and string, traverse boards were especially handy because most sailors couldn't read or write but were able to use them.

Each traverse board had two major parts. First, the **compass rose** on the top had 32 points arranged in a circle to mark cardinal direction.

compass rose

traverse board

There were eight rings of pegs for each of the 32 directions. Sailors started near the middle of the circle, then worked their way out, placing a peg in the hole every half hour for each observation.

The lower section of the traverse board, sometimes called the speed table, was for marking the speed of the ship. Sailors worked from left to right and kept track of how fast the ship was traveling. At the end of their four-hour watch, the sailor would know how far the ship had traveled and in what direction. If you were on a literate top-notch ship, the sailor on watch transcribed information into a log and maybe marked it on a chart.

Sailors improved on the heave log with the addition of a weight and a rope. The **chip log** was much easier to handle, and some sailors still use a version of it to this day. Introduced in the 1500s, the chip log consisted of a massive wooden spool holding an even more massive length of rope. Traditional chip logs from this era of navigation usually held 500 fathoms of rope—that's the old sailor's way of saying 3,000 feet (914m).

At the end of the rope was a carefully designed triangular weight with holes drilled into it to let water pass through. To determine the speed, the weight was dropped off the stern (back) of the ship. As the weight moved away from the ship, one sailor held the rope. Here's the most important part: On the rope, knots were always tied in equal distances apart from one another, usually around 50 feet per rope knot.

Just like a heave log, one sailor counted the knots passing by while another sailor watched the time using a sandglass. Sailors measured for just 30 seconds. Every knot of rope that passed in those 30 seconds counted as a mile per hour. For example, if you count three rope knots in 30 seconds, you're sailing at 3 knots, or 3 nautical miles per hour. (This is where the measurement of speed called "knots" came from.) With this quicker way to figure out speed, dead reckoning got a lot easier.

MAKE YOUR OWN MINI–CHIP LOG

Who needs a speedometer when you can make one yourself? This activity can be done on land or at a flowing creek or river. (If you're going the water route, be sure to bring an adult.)

SUPPLIES NEEDED: an empty paper towel roll; a marker; scissors; string, twine, or rope (the longer the better, but ideally 100 feet, or 30.5m); a plastic milk jug; a tape measure; and some water.

Part 1: Making the Chip Log

1. Find the middle of your empty paper towel roll and mark the spot with the marker.

2. Use the scissors to very carefully cut a narrow slit where you made your mark. Ensure that it's large enough to pass your string or rope through.

3 Bring one end of your rope through the hole and tie a simple double knot. Boom, you've got your spool and line ready to go.

4 Tie the opposite end of the rope to the handle of the milk jug.

5 Now it's time to mark our "knots." Starting on the milk jug end of the rope, use the tape measure and marker to mark every 22 feet (6.7m).

6 Finally, fill your milk jug with water to weigh it down if you're using your chip log on land. If you're heading to a creek, keep it empty.

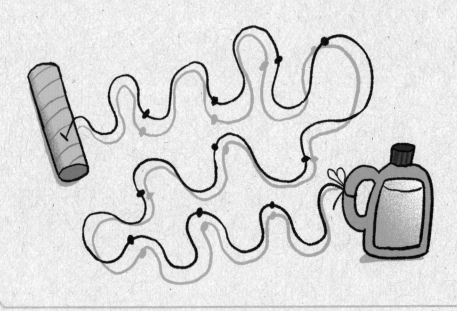

Part 2: Start Measuring

Note: To measure your speed in miles, use 15-second intervals for the 22-foot knots.

 Have your friend hold the jug and use a stopwatch (or count Mississippis) to time 15 seconds.

2 Carefully roll your rope up on the spool. Hold your spool loosely so the rope can unwind easily.

3 Walk away to measure speed. Be sure to count your knots! (If you're measuring the flow of water, place your jug in the stream and count your knots as the jug floats downstream.)

4 When time is called, the number of knots is how fast you walked away (or how fast the stream is moving) in miles per hour.

Epic Expeditions

Here are just a few of the journeys across oceans that had a major impact on the world and made history.

1325–1349: Moroccan scholar and explorer Ibn Battuta leaves home at age 21 for a pilgrimage to the Muslim Holy Land of Mecca. It turns into a nearly 30-year trip across parts of Africa, Asia, and Europe, spanning 75,000 miles (120,000km). Luckily for historians, he wrote a detailed (and factual) account of his travels.

1433: Zheng He leads the last Chinese maritime expedition before foreign trade is banned in his country. He reaches as far as Madagascar, trading goods on the coasts of East Africa and India along the way.

1473: Lopo Gonçalves of Portugal becomes the first European to sail below the equator. Europeans at the time believed that the sea at the equator was boiling hot, an idea he proved wrong.

1492: Christopher Columbus reaches the so-called New World, making landfall in the present-day Bahamas. He thought it was India.

1497–1500: John Cabot hits Newfoundland in present-day Canada; João Fernandes makes landfall nearby in what becomes known as Labrador; Columbus sails south to South America and *still* believes he's found the eastern edge of Asia!

1502: Amerigo Vespucci completes his second journey to South America. He argues correctly that the New World is indeed a landmass entirely separate from Asia. Amerigo will get two whole continents named after him.

1519–1522: Ferdinand Magellan captains the first lap around the earth—well, almost. He found a passage to the Pacific Ocean near the southern tip of South America (through the Strait of Magellan), but he died in battle in the Philippines. His crew made it back to Europe via the Cape of Good Hope.

1766–1769: Jeanne Baret becomes the first woman to circumnavigate the globe. Women weren't allowed on French navy ships in this period, so Baret disguised herself as a teenage boy. Working on board the *Étoile* as a botanist (a person who studies plants), she deceived the crew for over a year before her true identity was discovered in Tahiti.

UNRAVELING KNOTS, NAUTICAL MILES, AND THE 360-DEGREE EARTH

Not all miles are the same distance. The ones we use for air and sea travel, called **nautical miles**, are different in length from the **land miles** you run in a race or count off on the highway. Here's how we created two distinct but useful units for measuring distance.

Land miles (also called statute miles) are a randomly chosen length of 5,280 feet (1,609m). The mile was first based on the ancient Roman unit for 1,000 paces (1 pace was equal to 5 Roman feet), or *mille passus* in Latin. The mile the US uses today, however, originated in England around 1300. The government wanted to standardize measurements and decided to use the furlong, which originally measured out how far a team of oxen could plow a field without stopping for a break. There are 660 feet in a furlong, so the English decided on eight furlongs in a mile, or 5,280 feet.

Different societies around the world had their own definitions of a mile. For example, a Norwegian mile equaled around seven English miles. It wasn't until 1959 that the mile as we know it was standardized.

Nautical miles, on the other hand, are based on the actual size of the earth and how it's laid out, according to a 360-degree system. With the earth sliced in half at the equator, we have a circle, or **circumference**— 360 degrees of earth-y goodness. Measuring circles with 360 degrees can be traced all the way back to the ancient Egyptians, who inherited their sexagesimal number system (that means it's based on the number 60) from the Mesopotamians who came before them. Known lovers of a good triangle, the Egyptians noted that 6 perfect triangles fit in a circle—and 60 multiplied by 6 is 360.

Measuring distance using the size of the earth is much more useful for navigation. Here's how it works: With our planet cut in half at the equator like an orange, we can divide the earth into 360 degrees.

Northern
Hemisphere

Equator
= 360°

0° 30° 60° 90° 120° 150°

Southern
Hemisphere

Within each of those degrees are 60 **minutes of arc**. These minutes don't measure time—they measure distance. One minute of arc is a nautical mile. One nautical mile is equal to about 1.15 statute miles (or exactly 1,852 meters), and there are 60 nautical miles in every degree of latitude.

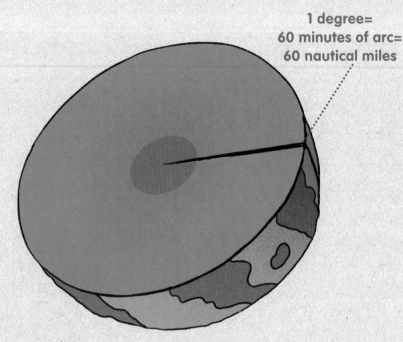

1 degree=
60 minutes of arc=
60 nautical miles

The nautical mile isn't just another unit of measure to get confused over. It's actually one of the most practical systems of determining distance that humans have ever dreamed up. As navigators continued to perceive the need to create a grid system (latitude and longitude) to measure the earth, nautical miles made reading distances and following the progress of journeys much faster. Instead of fussing over converting miles from every country's different system, a navigator could quickly consider their route in terms of degrees and minutes of arc. It's an objective system—think of it as the universal language of distance.

AN IMPERFECT SPHERE

This blue ball floating through space isn't a ball at all—it's an oblate spheroid. Thanks to some flattening at the poles, the earth isn't perfectly round. That causes all sorts of minor complications for navigation, one of which is determining nautical miles.

At the poles, a nautical mile is about 60 feet (18.3m) longer than at the equator. The world's solution? Average them out. It wasn't until 1970 that the whole world started using the same standard!

DIY PACE COUNT BEADS

It's time to use the principles of dead reckoning on land to measure your distance. You'll be tracking your walking paces with an old-school tool: pace count beads. This gadget is used by everyone from outdoor adventurers to Army rangers.

SUPPLIES NEEDED: a fresh 100-meter pack of twine, yarn, or rope (you can also use a running track with 100 meters marked out or an American football field including one end zone); a shoelace or paracord at least 12 inches (30.5cm) long; 15 beads (or anything you can thread your cord through, like metal nuts or washers); a pen; and some paper.

Part 1: Measure Out a Distance

1 We'll measure using meters rather than feet to make things simpler. Start by tying one end of the twine or rope to a sturdy object like a fence post.

2 Start a steady walking pace at the beginning of the 100-meter rope and count your paces. (Remember, a full pace is when *both* feet take a step.)

3 Now that you've got your pace count, you know you'll cover 100 meters in that many paces.

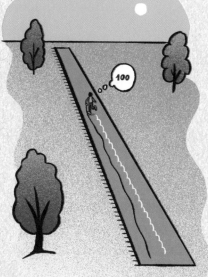

Since you've got to count every other step, it can be a lot of keep track of in your head—especially if you're in the woods. That's where the pace bead tool comes in. It works like this. There are two sets of beads on your tool: a set of nine beads and a set of five beads. The nine beads each represent 100 meters walked. After 900 meters, the next bead you move is from the five-bead set—that marks 1,000 meters, or one kilometer. Then you start over with the nine-bead set. The pace bead tool helps you easily track up to five kilometers traveled. Now let's make one.

ACTIVITY

Part 2: Make Your Pace Bead Tool

1 Fold your shoelace or paracord in half so it's twice as thick. You may need to experiment with the thickness of your cord, depending on the size of your beads. The beads should stay in place and not slide around or you could lose track of your paces!

2 Slide five beads onto one end of the cord. Tie a simple double or overhand knot at the near end of the cord so they don't slide off.

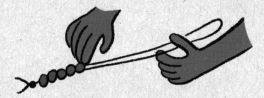

3 Tie another double knot about a third of the way from the stopped end to keep the beads in this section.

4 Add the other nine beads to the cord through the open end.

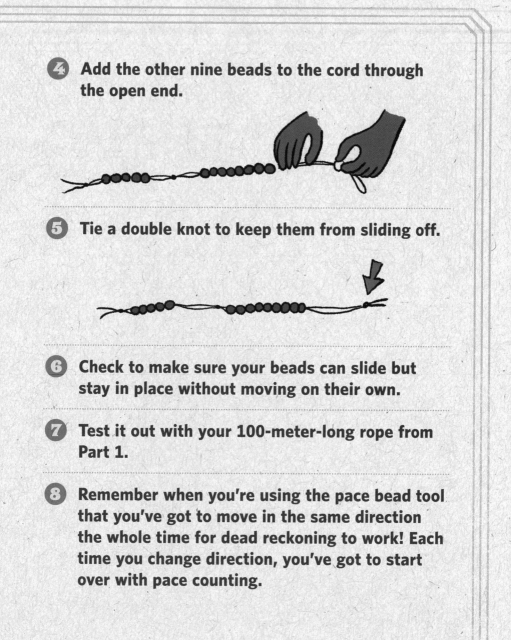

5 Tie a double knot to keep them from sliding off.

6 Check to make sure your beads can slide but stay in place without moving on their own.

7 Test it out with your 100-meter-long rope from Part 1.

8 Remember when you're using the pace bead tool that you've got to move in the same direction the whole time for dead reckoning to work! Each time you change direction, you've got to start over with pace counting.

Lewis and Clark
HALL OF FAME DEAD RECKONERS

Famed explorers Meriwether Lewis and William Clark made the first expedition across the western United States by non-Indigenous navigators in 1803. They used a variety of navigational techniques, including dead reckoning. Lewis and Clark were on a mission to map the United States' newly acquired lands and find a route to the Pacific coast. Along the route, they met and hired a teenage girl named Sacagawea to be their translator and guide. A member of the Lemhi Shoshone tribe, Sacagawea helped

the expedition communicate with the Indigenous peoples they encountered and was crucial to the group's mission.

On the journey, Clark developed sharp dead reckoning skills and was a fastidious notetaker. He made sure to keep careful records of their speed and traveling times to calculate distance. According to today's maps, Clark was only 40 miles (64km) off in his calculations of how far they traveled on the nearly 5,000-mile (8,046km) trip.

Knowing the fundamentals of dead reckoning can definitely come in handy on land. Whether you're lost in the woods, or bad weather makes seeing landmarks impossible, dead reckoning is a useful tool for any adventurer.

UNSURE ABOUT YOUR DEAD RECKONING? DEFINITELY DEAD

When everything goes well, dead reckoning can be simple and really helpful. But as any navigator will tell you, things don't always go according to plan. Strong weather might throw off your readings. The rope on your chip log could break or stretch. An unseen current could create a drift that affects the ship's speed. And there's always plenty of room for human error.

Getting lost due to poor dead reckoning could make long journeys even longer. With limited rations and poor food to begin with, the infamous vitamin C deficiency called scurvy could set in after about four weeks at sea. An estimated 2 million sailors died of scurvy during the Age of European Exploration. Mutinies were common, especially when the navigation of the ship was in doubt and food was running low.

The mood might have been getting mutinous on 21 Royal Navy ships in 1707 as the officers debated their position off the coast of southwestern England. Between 1,400 and 2,000 sailors died when six of the ships struck the cliffs of the rocky Isles of Scilly. Four ships sank altogether.

The disaster was due to a series of storms and poor dead reckoning. By the time the fleet realized they were far off course, it was too late. The incident was one of many navigational disasters during the era. Explorers seeking their fortunes needed more reliable methods of finding their way.

Dead reckoning wasn't going to cut it forever, and the British government was fed up with losing ships, sailors, and lost opportunities for wealth. So, in 1714, the British government offered a prize to whoever could solve the problem that had frustrated navigators for nearly a thousand years: determining longitudinal positioning at sea. The winner, they rightly believed, would make them a naval superpower for centuries. In the next chapter, we'll explore that story and why a seaworthy clock is a sailor's best friend.

FINDING LONGITUDE

HIGH TECH HITS THE HIGH SEAS

-4-

E very patch of the planet's 197-million-square-mile (510-million-km^2) surface can be pinpointed to within about four inches (10cm) using our grid system of latitude and longitude. It's an astoundingly accurate and simple way of accomplishing a job that's almost too big to comprehend.

As far as we know, the idea of mapping the world through latitude and longitude dates back to 250 BCE. Greek astronomer and mathematician Eratosthenes earned the nickname the "Father of Geography" for good reason. He used the basic tools around him to determine the circumference of the earth (24,901 miles, or 40,075km). Eratosthenes's next brilliant idea was a series of lines called parallels stacked above and below the equator and lines called **meridians** running north-south from pole to pole. Meridians use 360 degrees, just like parallels, and they range from 180 degrees east to 180 degrees west.

These imaginary lines that crisscross the globe are the foundation of modern navigation. We've already learned how to find our latitude (position north or south of the equator) using the stars. Even though this geographic coordinate system dates back to the ancient Greeks, it wasn't until the 18th century that navigators were able to find their east-west position of longitude at sea.

Part of the reason determining longitude is so difficult is because we live on a rotating planet. If the earth was just hanging out motionless in space, we could simply use two known stars to find our longitudinal position. Of course, that's not the case—polestars help us find our latitude, but there's no easy fix for longitude. Navigators needed to find a solution.

THE PRIME MERIDIAN

Countries didn't always agree where these lines of longitude would go in the first place. Deciding that the equator would be the starting point of 0 degrees for latitude was a no-brainer. That's because the equator is the midway point between the North and South

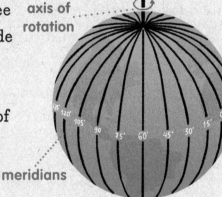

axis of rotation

meridians

Poles. The poles mark the top and bottom of the earth's **axis of rotation**, or the imaginary line through the middle of the planet along which it spins.

Deciding where to place 0 degrees of longitude, known as the **prime meridian**, was much harder—there are no East and West Poles for it to run through the middle of. Theoretically, the prime meridian could be any line of longitude placed anywhere. So where to put it?

Throughout history, astronomers and navigators have placed the prime meridian in countless locations. Once leaders caught on that the prime meridian could essentially be anywhere—it went, well, everywhere. It's estimated there were more than 20 different prime meridians in use around the world. Good luck asking anyone for directions if they're not using the same map as you!

By the mid-1700s, seafaring nations were dependent on their ability to safely navigate the high seas. With commerce going global, there was a serious need to get on the same page. The world's most powerful nations wanted to choose an official prime meridian and decide where east meets west.

It came down to a vote. On October 13, 1884, representatives from 25 countries got together and debated the issue at the International Meridian Conference. Longitude was a pressing matter, but so was the increasingly complicated issue of time. Without a standard system of time called **time zones** throughout the world, navigation was much more difficult. With new railways that extended across the expanding United States and stitched together countries in Europe, train travel was a complete mess.

A year before the conference, the United States had adopted four time zones, with Britain's Greenwich Mean Time (GMT) as the prime meridian. The meridian

TIME TWILIGHT ZONES

We know that true time is determined by the sun. But the reading on the clock is entirely up to the people in charge of where the clock is hanging. Here are three weird time zone quirks from around the world.

① THE TRANS-SIBERIAN RAILWAY:

From Moscow to Vladivostok you'll cross seven time zones and over 6,152 miles (9,900km) of Russian countryside, but the time will never change. The train cars and clocks at every station along the way all run on Moscow time.

for GMT passes through the Royal Observatory on the outskirts of East London. GMT offered one solution for standardizing longitude and time zones, but not every country was on board (or even at the table). Most notably, France was concerned that placing such an important designation in a rival superpower like Britain would give them an edge. Plus, France's own Paris Meridian ran

2 CHINA STANDARD TIME:
China is the third-largest country in the world by land area and crosses five time zones, but all 1.4 billion people use the same China Standard Time. That's led to some "unofficial" time zones in the western reaches of the country, where the sun officially sets around midnight in the summer.

3 VENEZUELA'S LEGAL TIME:
In 2007, President Hugo Chávez of Venezuela looked to leave his mark when he pushed back the country's time zone by 30 minutes. The following president, Nicolás Maduro, reversed the change less than a decade later.

through the heart of the city. Ultimately, Greenwich was made the international prime meridian.

The impact of playing host to the prime meridian clearly comes with its advantages. Even if it's just an imaginary line dividing east and west, determining time for the rest of the world lends power. After all, every map and clock depends on you!

Finding Longitude with Solar Noon

We can use time and the sun's position to help us figure out our longitude while navigating. Solar noon is the moment in which the sun reaches its highest point for the day at a given longitude. Most often it doesn't happen at exactly noon (12:00) local time, though usually it's pretty close.

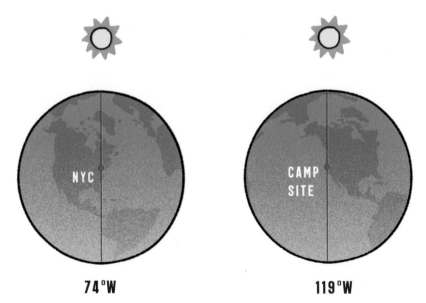

NYC

74°W

CAMP SITE

119°W

We know the earth makes one full rotation every 24 hours. Each rotation moves through 360 degrees of longitude. That means each hour the sun's highest point (solar noon) moves 15 degrees in longitude (because 360 degrees ÷ 24 hours = 15 degrees).

Here's an example. Our watch is set to local time at our home base in New York City, where solar noon is at exactly 12:00. As soon as we travel east or west of NYC, solar noon will be either before or after noon on our watch. We hop on a plane and fly thousands of miles west, where we'll find solar noon the next day in our new location (let's call it the camp site).

At the camp site, we set up our handy stick measuring system (more on that later) to find solar noon at that longitude. When solar noon happens at the camp site, our watch (still set to New York time) reads 3:00 p.m. That means solar noon happened three hours ago in NYC. So we traveled 45 degrees in longitude west of NYC. (Remember, solar noon moves 15 degrees per hour, so that's 15 + 15 + 15 = 45).

With New York City's longitude of 74 degrees west, we add 45 degrees to put us at about 119 degrees west. (74 degrees + 45 degrees = 119 degrees.) Presto, we have our location!

TRACK THE SUN!

Let's track and locate (roughly) where noon is at any time of day!

SUPPLIES NEEDED: an accurate watch, a globe or map, sticky notes, and a pen.

1 Mark where you live (home base) on the map with a sticky note. Your home base's meridian is now the prime meridian. Congratulations, time revolves around you now!

2 Based on the time at home base, count the number of hours until it will be noon. Or if noon has already passed today, count the hours since noon.

3 We know that the sun moves at 15 degrees of longitude per hour. Using the information from Step 2, about how many degrees away is noon?

4 Predict where noon will be in five hours and use another sticky note to place it on the map. How about 10 hours?

5 You can check to see if your results were correct with an internet search.

SOLVING THE
LONGITUDE PROBLEM

Since the early days of celestial navigation, the problem
of finding an east-west position of longitude perplexed
the greatest minds on earth. Latitude was easy enough to
sort out with our trusty polestars to guide us. But it would
take thousands of years of observation, record keeping,
and tinkering before navigators could figure out their
longitudinal positions.

One particularly famous astronomer thought he had
the perfect fix for longitude when he noticed a curious
pattern around Jupiter. In 1610, Galileo was doing some
stargazing with his fancy self-built telescope from his

balcony in Padua, Italy. He noticed four moons orbiting Jupiter with such consistency that he could set his watch to their movements. Problem solved, right? Not so fast. Using Jupiter's moons worked well with an advanced telescope and a steady surface to set it up on. On a ship, however, using a telescope powerful enough to spot the moons was near impossible and the method still required long calculations.

NO BAD IDEAS? (OKAY, HERE'S AN OBJECTIVELY BAD IDEA)

The Wounded Dog Theory of determining longitude surely ranks among the worst ideas put forth. Around 1687, a very fake medicine called Powder of Sympathy could supposedly heal from any distance. It was getting popular in France, and some thought it could be used for navigation, too.

The theory went like this: Put a wounded dog on a ship and leave a bandage from the dog's wound at port. Every hour, the "healer" at port would place the bogus magic powder on the bandage, inspiring a yelp from the dog and notifying the sailors of the passage of time at port. Not surprisingly, this didn't catch on and there aren't wide reports of sailors testing it. Can you blame them?

Solutions to the longitude problem were coming along, but far too slowly for the British government's liking. They decided to jumpstart the process in 1714 by founding the Commissioners for the Discovery of the Longitude at Sea. The group was composed of the country's leaders across politics, commerce, and science. They had one goal: Solve the longitude problem once and for all.

Noting that their original name was a bit longwinded, the group became known as the Board of Longitude. Most people, however, were really just interested in the prize they were offering. If an inventor's device or methods could determine the longitude of a ship within 30 nautical miles, they would receive a prize of 20,000 pounds sterling. That's around 4 million pounds or 5.2 million US dollars today—not bad!

There were two popular routes to solving the problem. The first was called the lunar distance method, which meant improving the tables (charts) that predicted the movement of celestial bodies. The second was creating a clock that could keep time on a turbulent ship for months on end. Both solutions presented huge barriers to overcome, but the clock problem in particular had its serious doubters. The godfather of gravity himself, Sir Isaac Newton, thought that a clock that could keep time on a ship was a near impossibility. The world's curious navigators and inventors got to work, and as luck would have it, the two lasting solutions were fine-tuned in the same year, 1761.

THE LUNAR DISTANCE METHOD

Self-taught German cartographer (or mapmaker) Johann Tobias Mayer spent more than a decade refining tables for predicting the moon's movements relative to the stars. With his super-accurate findings, Mayer devised a system that used the angle of the moon and a known star to determine longitude.

By this time, a measuring instrument called the **octant** was widely used. Using a double reflection system, the navigator could measure the angle between two celestial bodies—like the moon and a star, as Mayer's method suggested. Here's how it works.

Mayer realized that finding longitude is all about time. Imagine the stars in the sky are like the numbers on a clock face while the moon acts as the moving hour hand. From the ship, the navigator judges the moon's **altitude**, or the angle between the moon and the horizon.

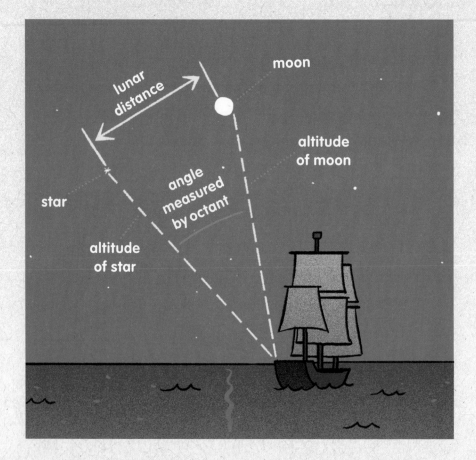

The navigator then measures the altitude of a known star and calculates the angle between them.

These values were then plugged into the star tables—and hopefully you didn't pick up a shabby bootleg copy. The tables would tell the navigator at what time the stars were in that same position over a prime meridian. Then, by determining the ship's local time, they could find their relationship to time at the prime meridian.

Okay, this all might sound like a whole lot of work, but it was a major step forward. The accuracy of the tables seriously impressed the Board of Longitude, who were ready to give the grand prize to Mayer. Unfortunately, Mayer died before the good news arrived. His widow received a small portion of the prize, just 3,000 pounds.

Meanwhile, a new type of clock was shattering scientists' notions of what was possible. It seemed the longitude problem might be finally solved far from the halls of power in Greenwich by a no-name clockmaker from a dingy town in Yorkshire, England.

THE FIRST-EVER MARINE CHRONOMETER

Navigators understood that time was the key to determining their longitude. They had already figured out that the sun moved 15 degrees of longitude per hour. If they could accurately keep time from their home port, they would know how far east or west they had traveled based on the time difference between solar noon at home and solar noon in their new location.

The problem was that the delicate clocks of the day were all likely to lose time if they were moved or even sneezed at. Pendulum clocks relied on the swinging momentum of a weight to stay accurate—not the best match for sailing the open sea on a rolling ship.

THE WORLD'S MOST USEFUL ROLEX

Known more for their price tag than usefulness, the Rolex GMT watch features a second hour hand that tracks GMT with a rotating bezel (the ring around the watch face). Originally developed for airline pilots, this is one of history's more stylish (and pricey) longitude-tracking tools.

Clearly a different approach was needed and the man for the job was John Harrison. A self-taught clockmaker and carpenter from humble beginnings, Harrison was something of a restless inventor. While the rest of the world used brass fittings for their pendulum clocks, he made them entirely out of wood—the material he knew best as a carpenter.

Harrison's wood clocks lost only around one second per month while high-end brass clocks lost about a minute per day. This is partly because his clocks didn't have to be greased—any part needing lubrication was made from a tropical hardwood containing its own natural oils.

Harrison's incredible patience and tendency to think differently about solving problems set him apart from others seeking the longitude prize. The first clock he submitted, dubbed the H1, ditched the problematic pendulum design. It took him five years to construct it. A partial success, the clock kept time on half of its round-trip journey to Portugal in 1736.

H1   H2   H3

After another three years of development, Harrison's second clock, H2, was ready. But Harrison noticed a flaw in his design. He had accounted for the rocking and turbulent seas, but not for the sweeping movement that ships make when they quickly turn to catch the wind. The setback was difficult but didn't break Harrison's spirit.

H3 took a whopping 19 years of full-time dedication. Weighing 60 pounds and standing more than two feet (0.6m) high, the clock had exactly 753 parts. But the springs inside it still couldn't manage the rocking of a ship.

H3 was the last marine clock Harrison would build. That's when he really got cooking with H4. He made a radical design change away from big, clock-style devices and toward a circular **chronometer** design that was more like a pocket watch. Chronometers are a special type of time-keeping tool.

HARRISON'S WORLD RECORD

Roasted by his peers as outrageous, Harrison's designs were clearly ahead of their time. In 2015, 250 years after Harrison designed a land clock called Clock B, a group of watchmakers put his plans to work. The clock set a Guinness World Record and was accurate up to one second over 100 days.

Unlike clocks, they're light, portable, and can keep time while getting battered around. But they also need to keep time with serious precision. Back in Harrison's era, even the best pocket watches were usually off by at least an hour at the end of the day.

What really set H4 apart though was the **higher frequency movement**. The movement in this term refers to the mechanism that keeps the device ticking. A high frequency movement chronometer features parts that are smaller but spin more rotations to keep time.

Six years after scrapping the H3, the H4 was ready for its test. In 1761, around the same time as Johann Mayer was sending his groundbreaking celestial charts to the board, the HMS *Deptford* set sail for Kingston, Jamaica, with Harrison's son keeping watch over the H4's journey.

The trial was a success. Harrison's fourth version only lost five seconds on the journey, and the longitude reading was accurate to within one nautical mile. His watch was even more accurate than the prize demanded. The board, however, refused to award Harrison the 20,000-pound prize. After appealing directly to King George III, Harrison finally received the money that was owed to him, but he didn't get the actual distinction of the prize. No one ever did.

Harrison's watch emerged as the simplest way to determine longitude. In a matter of decades there were thousands of producers of the marine chronometer, and they became an essential part of every captain's kit. In the 1770s, Captain James Cook praised the device. He used both the chronometer and lunar observation when he and the expert Polynesian navigator Tupaia mapped and explored the south Pacific.

Inside an H4 chromometer

While the marine chronometer and the lunar distance method were astounding steps forward for navigation, each had its trade-offs. The lunar method required long calculations and a good view of the moon and stars— not always possible in poor weather. Meanwhile, the marine chronometer was expensive. If it was lost, broken, or stolen you were back to dead reckoning. That's why, like all tools and navigation skills, the more of them you know the more likely you'll get to your destination.

FIND SOLAR NOON (AND YOUR LONGITUDE)

We previously used a stick to find our direction, but determining longitude takes precision. A minute's difference could throw you off as much as 17 miles (27.4km) at the equator!

> **SUPPLIES NEEDED:** a flat work space that gets good sunlight, a clock or watch, a cardboard box with a flat top and bottom, one long nail, a ruler, Scotch tape, a few pieces of plain construction paper, a pencil, and a world map (online or in a book).

Part 1: Measure Solar Noon

1 Set up your observation space about an hour before 12:00 p.m. You'll need unobstructed sunlight for this to work.

2 Make sure your surface is flat. (Most smartphones have a level tool you can use.)

3 Tape any openings on your cardboard box so it rests flat on your workspace and the top of the box is flat.

4 Center your construction paper on the top of your box and tape the corners in place.

5 Gently press the nail through the center of your stack of paper. Make sure it's sticking straight up and not slanted.

6 On your paper, mark the end of the nail's shadow and write the clock time above it.

7 Check the shadow's position every 10 minutes. Mark each position and clock time.

8 Around 30 minutes before clock noon, start marking the time every five minutes. The shadows should be getting closer together.

9 It's crunch time, so stay on top of the data collection! Solar noon lands at different times throughout the year—it's earlier in winter and later in summer.

10 Watch closely. If the shadows are still getting closer together, you haven't reached solar noon yet. As the shadows narrow to within one finger's width, mark the time every minute.

11 Once the shadows begin getting farther from the nail, we've passed solar noon. Solar noon's mark is the one closest to the nail.

12 Pull the nail out of the paper and grab your ruler. Line the edge up with the hole from your nail.

13 Once you've found the shortest shadow, you've found the time for solar noon in your exact spot!

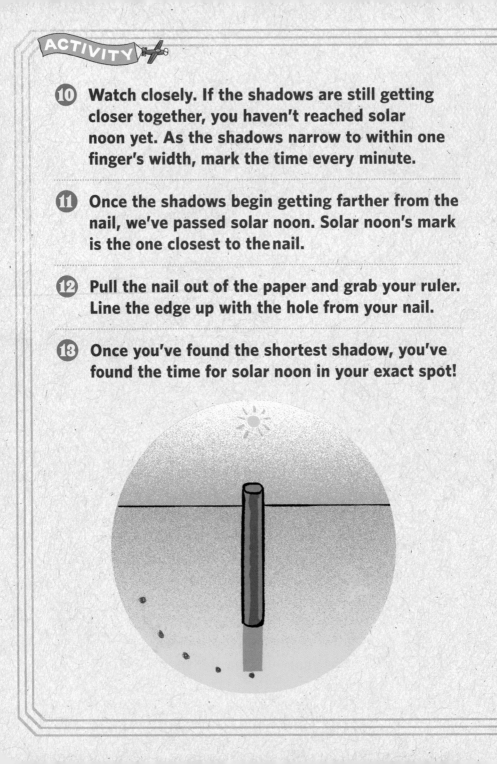

Part 2: Quick and Easy-ish Longitude

Now it's time to figure out your longitude. Since you probably don't have an H4 marine chronometer already set to Greenwich time, let's make one!

1 **Grab an accurate watch that you can change the time on.**

2 **Determine the time in Greenwich. Look it up on the internet, or use a world map to check how many hours (time zones) you are east or west of the prime meridian in Greenwich. Change your watch to Greenwich time—you've now got the most influential navigational tool in history.**

3 **With the solar noon reading you found in Part 1 of this activity, determine how many hours and minutes you are ahead of or behind noon in Greenwich. (For this example, solar noon in Greenwich for today is noon on the dot.)**

4 **Multiply the number of hours by 15. Then multiply the number of minutes by 0.25. Add those answers together.**

5 **Your total is the number of degrees you are (roughly) east or west of the prime meridian.**

-5-
FOLLOW THE NEEDLE

THE ALMIGHTY MAP AND COMPASS

Pound for pound, you'd be hard-pressed to find a gadget that's been more influential on the course of human history than the compass. Weighing virtually nothing and discovered in part by chance, compasses use the earth's magnetic poles to find your cardinal direction. Compasses are still among the world's most useful navigation tools. But compared to celestial navigation, they haven't been widely used for very long.

So what makes compasses so helpful? Use it correctly and it will give you your **bearing**—the cardinal direction you're traveling, expressed in degrees. In this chapter we'll cover some of the history of the compass and witness its magnetic magic at work (thanks, Earth!). Then we'll touch on how using the compass really makes for some reliable navigating. Finally, we'll look at some of the maps you might come into contact with and how to use them with a compass.

EARTH'S PROTECTIVE AND POWERFUL MAGNETIC FIELDS

You probably know already that magnets are super-fun to play around with. Well, guess what? The earth itself is a gigantic magnet. Every magnet, including Earth, has a north pole and south pole at opposite ends. An invisible area called a **magnetic field** surrounds all magnets and either pulls in (attracts) or pushes away (repels) other magnetic objects. The poles are attracted to their opposites: north to south, and south to north.

With a compass, we can use the earth's magnetism to point us in the right direction while navigating. Since the earth is one giant magnet—with one side of polarity in the north and the other in the south—the magnetized needle of a compass is attracted to the opposite pole. The needle's south pole points to the earth's North Pole

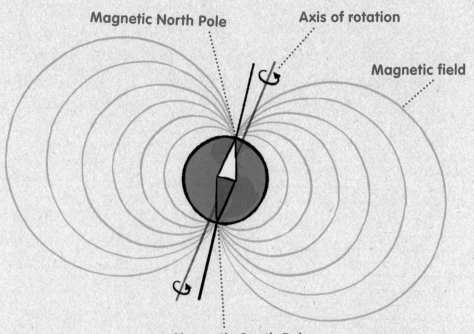

Magnetic North Pole

Axis of rotation

Magnetic field

Magnetic South Pole

(its magnetically polar opposite). Imagine a rectangular magnet lying from pole to pole—the top of the magnet at the North Pole would have south polarity as it attracts the north side of the needle.

About every 200 to 300 thousand years, the earth's polarity flips, doing a complete 180-degree turn. But the earth's magnetic field doesn't exactly keep a regular schedule. It's been more than 700 thousand years since the last polarity flip.

THE AURORAS

Solar winds whipping off the sun release an estimated seven billion tons of particles an hour. Fortunately, the magnetic field around the earth acts as a sort of force field protecting us from this solar matter.

The few bits that do get through collide with atmospheric gases to create a dazzling light show called the auroras. In the Northern Hemisphere it's known as aurora borealis or the northern lights. In the Southern Hemisphere it's called aurora australis or the southern lights.

So what makes the earth magnetic? Well, it's all thanks to the metals inside our planet, which has a 1,000-degree inner core of solid iron and nickel. There are several layers surrounding that core.

The outer core, located 1,800 miles (2,897km) beneath our feet, creates this magnetic field that surrounds Earth like a bubble. The constant churning of an ocean of liquid iron in the outer core generates an electrical current that creates our planetary magnetism.

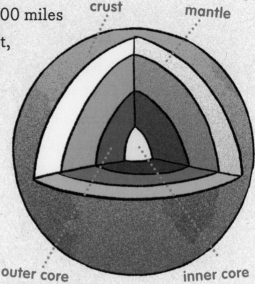

crust

mantle

outer core

inner core

HUMANS AND MAGNETISM: BETTER LATE THAN NEVER

As we saw back in Chapter 1, certain animals make use of the earth's magnetic field for navigation. Critters as small as fruit flies and as big as whales detect the poles in order to find mates, food, and their home base. Humans took a little bit longer to catch on to the push and pull of the earth's poles. It was only around 2,200 years ago that we first discovered how certain metals move to line up in a north-south direction—and the first known uses of that knowledge had nothing to do with navigation.

During the Han Dynasty in China between 206 BCE and 220 CE, a new tool for fortune-telling emerged that would change the world forever. The gadget was a special metal spoon made of magnetic ore. Fortune-tellers would place the flat-bottomed spoon on a bronze plate with etchings of constellations and the moon in its various phases arranged in a circle.

Even as the plate was moved to various locations and rotated, the spoon always lined up in a north-south position. It helped those practicing the technique to arrange everything from homes to the position of a funeral burial in line with the earth's magnetic field, which was believed to create harmony and good fortune. The spoons behaved the way they did because they were made of **lodestone**, one of the few materials on Earth that naturally has magnetic properties. Lodestone is a piece of a mineral called magnetite that has become magnetized. (Think of it like a superhero whose powers have come to life.)

Gradually, those using the lodestone spoons began to better understand its mysteries. By the 7th century CE, tinkerers from the Tang Dynasty in China learned how to transfer magnetic powers from lodestone to iron, a much more common material. By rubbing iron needles against lodestone, they could magnetize the iron as well. When set on a light piece of wood in a bowl of water, the needles would detect the pull of the earth's poles and orient themselves in a north-south line. Rather than telling fortunes, the lodestone device was now used to check directions at sea when the sun was nowhere to be seen.

By the 11th and 12th centuries, Chinese sailors were using full-blown compasses to navigate on journeys to Southeast Asia and west to the Persian Gulf and Africa. In the 13th century, famed Italian explorer Marco Polo traveled to China via the Silk Road (a network of trading routes connecting Europe, Asia, and Africa). He was among the first Europeans to visit East Asia and would go on to write extensively about his travels.

Polo lived in China for 17 years, where he served in the emperor's court. He later wrote an epic account of his travels and told of inventions like paper money, eyeglasses, and the burning of coal for fuel. Of course, historians now consider many of Polo's tales to be made up. But there's no doubt those stories inspired later European explorers like Christopher Columbus to find and exploit valuable resources in faraway lands.

It's unclear exactly how the compass spread between China and the rest of the world, but we do know that its use spread during the 13th century, after Polo returned to Europe from his journey. As more people started using the compass around the planet, compass designs changed based on who was using it and where.

The device eventually turned into what's called a card compass or **dry compass**. Without the resistance of the water in a bowl, the magnetized needle could move with greater ease. It was more precise, but bumps

in the ocean made the needle jump. Beneath the needle, a compass rose showed the cardinal directions and all their variations (a very hard-to-memorize 32 in total). Dry compasses were widely used in Asia and Europe by the 1300s. The new gadget allowed explorers like Ferdinand Magellan and Christopher Columbus to dead reckon their ways around the world.

The longer the voyages got, the more ornate the rose designs became. They varied by culture, too—in the Mediterranean, for example, east was often marked with a cross because it was the direction of Jerusalem (the Holy Land for Christians). Elsewhere in Europe, north was first marked with a *T* for Tramontane, the name of the north wind that blew in from over the Alps. It was later replaced by the royal fleur-de-lis symbol, a nod to the kings and queens who funded—and profited off of—many of the expeditions during the Age of European Exploration.

MAKE YOUR OWN COMPASS

This simple compass is an easy way to check directions—or to just impress your friends. When you're doing this one, keep in mind some of the factors that can disrupt the earth's magnetic fields, like metal, microwaves, phones, or watches. You'll want a tech-free workspace clear of metal.

SUPPLIES NEEDED: a paper clip, a Popsicle stick, a marker, a magnet (any kind), masking tape, a nonmetal bowl of water, and a milk jug lid.

1 Straighten your paper clip as best you can—it doesn't need to be totally perfect.

2 Put a mark on one tip of the Popsicle stick—we'll figure out which side is north and which is south later.

3 Lay your straightened paper clip on the stick.

4 Activate the magnetic superpowers of your paper clip by rubbing your magnet on the straightened paper clip. Start from the same end of the paper clip each time and only rub in one direction.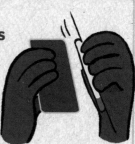

5 Tape the center of your paper clip to the Popsicle stick.

6 We're ready to use our compass. Set the milk jug lid in your bowl of water upside down so it floats.

7 Place your Popsicle stick on the lid with the paper clip facing up.

8 Now your compass is working for you—it should be pointing in a north-south direction.

9 To determine which way is north, use clues from the sun, stars, or nature.

10 You can double-check your directions using a smartphone's compass or a handheld compass and mark the Popsicle stick's north or south.

NAVIGATION MEETS RELIGION

Shortly after compasses arrived in the Muslim world, inventors developed models to show the direction of Mecca, known as the qibla. Around 1350, astronomer Ibn al-Shatir incorporated a simple sundial onto the qibla compass so worshippers would also know when to pray.

Since those early days, little has fundamentally changed in compass designs. Today's fancy, top-of-the-line compasses function by the same principles as those used in China long ago. The biggest improvements have been in the magnetism and stability of the needles, so compasses are easier to work with.

TWO NORTHS AND TWO SOUTHS: MAGNETIC DECLINATION

While it would be convenient for the geographic poles (the North Pole and South Pole) to line up neatly with the magnetic poles, our planet is a big, messy place. After all, we have a bubbling sea of liquid metal to thank for the whole magnetic field thing. Plus, that would make navigation too easy! Christopher Columbus noticed this inconsistency between geographic and magnetic poles during his first journey across the Atlantic in 1492.

A few days after leaving port, Columbus realized his compass needle wasn't pointing in the direction of Polaris—instead it was tilted farther west. Word got out to the ship's crew that the compass needle was behaving unpredictably, and he needed to act fast.

Columbus came up with an answer that was commonly believed in his day: that there were new, mysterious planets rotating somewhere off the North Pole. Could make for a great story, but what was really happening to the compass?

The compass on Columbus's ship was indicating the direction of the Magnetic North Pole (also called "magnetic north") and not the Geographic North Pole (known as "true north"). Magnetic north is the spot at the top of the magnet that is Earth. By the same token, the Magnetic South Pole is at the opposite end. Here's an easy way to remember: True north is always where it says it is on the map and never moves. Magnetic north shifts around—so keep an eye on it!

Both magnetic north and south are constantly moving due to the liquid metal moving around like crazy in the earth's outer core. Scientists estimate that the poles move about 30 miles (48km) per year. In 2019, however, magnetic north made such an unexpected and large jump that researchers made an earlier-than-usual adjustment to the measurement of maps and GPS systems so that they wouldn't be catastrophically inaccurate.

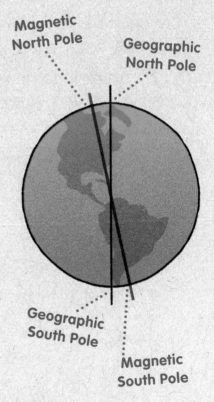

Magnetic North Pole

Geographic North Pole

Geographic South Pole

Magnetic South Pole

COMPASS KRYPTONITE

Not to be confused with declination, deviation is when a compass gets confused by another magnetic field—and there are lots of them. Metal objects like jewelry, wristwatches, pocketknives, and common electronics like phones and cameras will cause your needle to jump and leave you lost. Whether you're a pro or still learning, make sure your compass can work without interruptions.

Maps are usually oriented with true north in mind, so any time we use a compass, we need to account for the difference between true north and magnetic north. That difference is called **magnetic declination**. It varies depending on your location, and thanks to those shifty magnetic poles, it changes over time. Taking magnetic declination into account is absolutely essential for successful navigating. Fail to do so and you'll get lost!

★ ★ ★

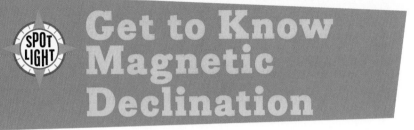

Get to Know Magnetic Declination

How could the position of your declination affect navigation? Let's investigate.

East-west positioning is super important when correcting for magnetic declination. It dictates which direction your compass needle is getting pulled in. If your magnetic north is east of true north, that means it's a positive declination. It's adding to your direction and pushing the needle farther east, so you need to subtract those extra degrees to get back to true north.

On the other hand, if magnetic north is west of true north, it's a negative declination. The compass needle is getting pulled over to the west, so you need to add the angle of declination in degrees to push it back to true north. Here's an easy way to remember: East is least (subtract), west is best (add).

Here's an example: We're looking to walk true north. We check the declination in our area using an up-to-date map or web resource and find it's 10 degrees west. From that, we know that magnetic north is pulling our compass needle west by 10 degrees. So, we add 10 degrees to our original bearing.

Reminder: Magnetic declination changes frequently. It's best to check out the declination of the area you want to explore *before* using your compass. You can find this information easily online. It's also usually listed on the bottom of local maps—just be sure your maps are up-to-date.

Baseplate compasses offer a feature that allows you to adjust them to your local declination. This is a great feature if you want to minimize the number of steps (and math) in your navigation, but it isn't necessary. Besides, an extra bit of math never killed anyone (well . . . let me double-check that).

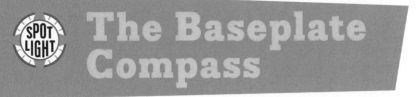

The Baseplate Compass

Used by adventurers the world over, this simple gadget can guide you through most terrain. Let's check out the components.

What's the most important part of any compass? The **1** needle, of course. Notice how the needle is split into two

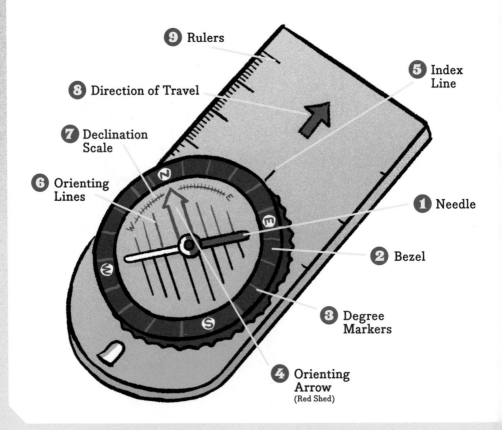

9 Rulers

8 Direction of Travel

7 Declination Scale

6 Orienting Lines

5 Index Line

1 Needle

2 Bezel

3 Degree Markers

4 Orienting Arrow
(Red Shed)

colors—the red side is north. Always. No matter where you are in the world the red end of the needle will point north.

Next up is the ❷ bezel. This is a useful ring that rotates in both directions and has ❸ degree markers for all 360 degrees. Due north is 0 degrees while east lies at 90, south at 180, and west at 270. As the bezel spins, so does the face beneath the needle. Within that face is a painted red box that works as an ❹ orienting arrow. Nicknamed "the red shed," it's a big part of what makes this type of compass so useful.

As we rotate the compass, the red side of the needle will always find magnetic north. To get a bearing, we need to line up this north-pointing needle with the red box. Here's an easy saying to remember: "red in the shed." Rotate the bezel until red is in the shed. Now you can get your bearing off the ❺ index line in the bezel. The same dial that houses the "red shed" also contains ❻ orienting lines—these help align us with true north on a map. And if your compass has a ❼ declination scale, twist it to adjust for magnetic declination.

At the top of your baseplate there's a small arrow— that's your ❽ direction of travel. Any time you're holding the compass to navigate, that arrow should be facing away from you. The ❾ rulers for centimeters and inches come in handy for tracking progress on maps.

VISUALIZING DECLINATION

Here's a quick way to see what a difference magnetic declination can make. This one can be done in any open space, but a sports field is best.

Note: Before you head outside, check the magnetic declination for your area. One of the best online resources is the US National Oceanic and Atmospheric Administration's (NOAA) Magnetic Field Calculator.

SUPPLIES NEEDED: your compass and three items to mark spots in the grass (like a hat, a sweater, and an extra jacket).

1 **Mark your starting point with a piece of clothing and set the bezel to 0 degrees.**

2 **Hold the compass flat and rotate your body until the red needle is in the shed. You're now facing the direction of magnetic north.**

3 Count out 50 paces and drop the second marker.

4 Return to your starting point and adjust your compass for your local declination.

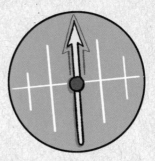

5 From the same place you started in Step 1, rotate your body and compass until "red is in the shed." This is the direction of true north.

6 Count 50 paces again and drop another marker. Are the two items of clothing far apart? Imagine how far your paths would be apart if you walked in that direction all day!

TAKE A BEARING IN THE WILD

Now that we've got the knowledge, it's time to put it to use. Let's take the bearing of a landmark. Working with a compass is best (and most fun) outside in the great outdoors. Find the best open space you can—anything from a city park to your backyard will do the trick.

SUPPLIES NEEDED: this book, the magnetic declination for your area (see page 154), a compass, and a friend you can show off to (or share this skill with).

1. Survey your surroundings and pick out a landmark somewhere in your field of vision.

2. Hold your compass flat in your hand so the needle can move freely and the direction of travel arrow on the baseplate is facing away from you.

3. Point the direction of travel arrow at the landmark and keep it locked on that position.

4. Hold the baseplate firmly and rotate the bezel until the needle is in the orienting arrow ("red in the shed").

5. Check the index line for your reading.

6. Correct for that pesky magnetic declination— remember east is least (rotate the bezel clockwise) and west is best (rotate the bezel counterclockwise).

7. Check the index line again. That's our bearing for the landmark.

MAXIMIZING MAPS

Whether they depict your neighborhood or the whole planet, maps are the most widely utilized navigation tools in the world. The most popular web mapping tool, Google Maps, has over one billion active users—that's about one in every seven people. Any map is far from perfect, however, and as the area it depicts gets bigger, so do the problems.

Simply put, the problems arise from taking a curved surface of a sphere (our planet) and attempting to make it flat. There are bound to be some distortions and inaccuracies. Today's most familiar world map, the 500-year-old **Mercator projection**, is no exception. It accounts for the difference by making Europe, North America, and Greenland much bigger than they actually are, while downsizing Africa and South America. It was a product of its time when Europeans saw North America as an emerging land to

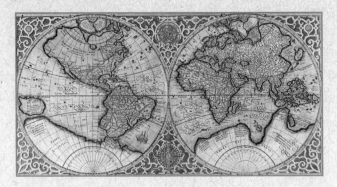

FLAT MAP, ROUND(ISH) EARTH

If your classmates don't believe that the flat map of all seven continents you've seen at school is wrong, try a quick experiment. Grab a white plastic bag, turn it inside out, and drop a basketball inside. Pull it tight against the ball to remove any wrinkles and do a quick drawing of the seven continents. Then take the ball out and flatten the bag. Did your representation change when they went from round to flat?

explore, exploit, and colonize. Today, the map's lasting popularity sadly shows how western cultures still often see themselves as the center of the world.

There's good news, however, for us compass-toting navigators. The smaller the area that a map portrays, the more detailed and accurate it is. This is called the **scale**, meaning the ratio between what's depicted on the map and its actual size. Ancient Chinese cartographers first developed maps drawn to scale around 200 BCE.

For example, a map with a scale of 1:24,000 means that one inch (2.5cm) on the map equals 24,000 inches (609m) in the real world. The scale will always be written in the map's **legend** (also known as the key), where every symbol's meaning is explained.

Scales are widely referred to as being large or small, but that can get confusing. Large-scale maps show a smaller space in greater detail while small-scale maps show larger areas in less detail. Large-scale maps, anywhere from 1:1,000 to 1:50,000, are great for walking and navigating with a compass. Meanwhile, medium- to small-scale maps in the 1:100,000 to 1:500,000 range are used for road maps, nautical navigation, and flying aircraft. Finally, the world maps that hang on your wall are in the 1:2,000,000 range!

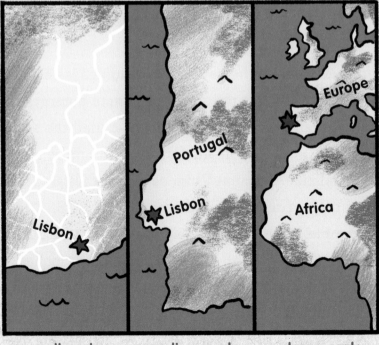

small-scale   medium-scale   large-scale

NAVIGATING FOR SPORT

Maps and compasses aren't just for getting around. Orienteering is a global sport where competitors race to different checkpoints using their navigation skills and speed. Originally started as a military exercise in Sweden around 1890, competitive orienteering is now popular around the world. The sport is done on foot, skis, and the latest—mountain bikes.

The most epic of all orienteering races is the 10-day Patagonian Expedition Race in South America. It covers more than 370 miles (600 km) of rugged mountains, ocean, and forests with only about 55 percent of teams finishing each year. Participants must bike, hike, paddle, and climb, all with their map, compass, and camping gear in tow. Many call it the world's most challenging race.

Now our knowledge of latitude and longitude comes into play. Maps are sometimes referred to by how many minutes they contain—and no, that's not how long it takes to cross them. The minutes of the map refer to the size of the area it covers. Three common sizes are 7.5, 15, and 30 minutes. Each minute accounts for 1.15 miles (1.85km) or one nautical mile, just like each minute of latitude.

Maps are packed with information, and at first they can be overwhelming. If we break down each component of a map, we see that each line and symbol has a specific purpose and story to tell. After you've determined the scale of the map, head to the legend. Think of it as the handbook for the map—most questions can be answered in or around the legend.

For exploring the wilderness, you'll want to get your hands on **topographic maps**. First developed by French cartographers in the 1700s, these maps are easy to find and perfect for navigating with a compass.

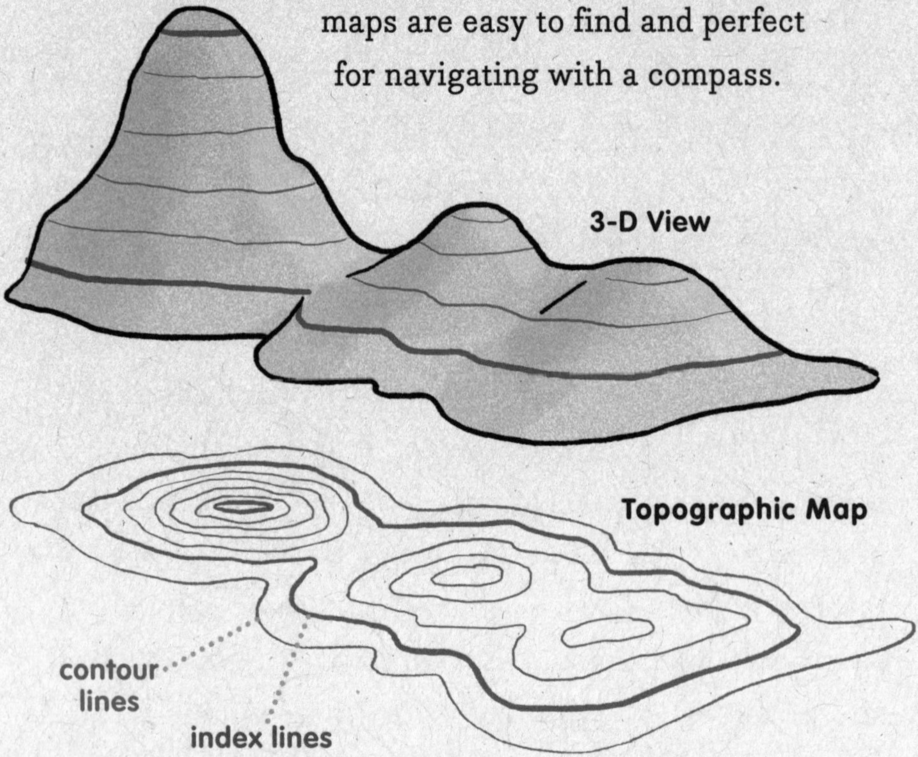

3-D View

Topographic Map

contour
lines

index lines

Topographic maps are especially useful in hilly terrain. You'll notice they have wavy lines that look sort of like fingerprints—those are called **contour lines** and they show changes in elevation. Each line represents a set number of feet found in the legend. Every fifth line is darker and contains a number. That's called your **index line** and offers a reading on the elevation. When the lines are closer together, it means the terrain is steeper.

Navigating with a map and compass takes practice, but once mastered it's a skill that will become second nature. There are a few things to check every time you use a map and compass. First, make sure that the top of the map is north. Some maps, especially in the Southern Hemisphere, are oriented with south at the top.

Next you'll find the local declination between magnetic north and true north—don't forget to adjust your compass. Remember that magnetic north is always cruising around, so make sure your map is no more than a few years old. Always use maps that are up-to-date and from a good source. Vintage maps are cool, but their place is at home on your wall or in a book, not in the field. Finally, bring an adult, a friend, and a phone when you're learning because getting lost isn't fun and it's even less fun alone!

Now let's put these map and compass skills to work.

TRIANGULATION

A map isn't very useful if you're not sure where you are on it. Take a moment to get oriented by finding your current position on the map. The fastest way to do this is by looking for nearby landmarks like peaks, rivers, lakes, roads, paths—anything will do. If you're really stuck, there's always triangulation, and we already have the skills we need to do it.

SUPPLIES NEEDED: your location's magnetic declination, a baseplate compass, a map of your area, and a pencil.

Part 1: Find Your Location

1 First things first—always adjust your compass for magnetic declination. East is least, west is best.

2 Remember when we learned to take the bearing of a landmark before we got our map? Start out by taking the bearing of a visible landmark.

3 Now lay down your map flat and make sure any metal objects (like a phone, watch, or pocket knife) are out of the way.

4 Line up the longer straight edge of your compass with the landmark—the direction of travel should be facing the landmark.

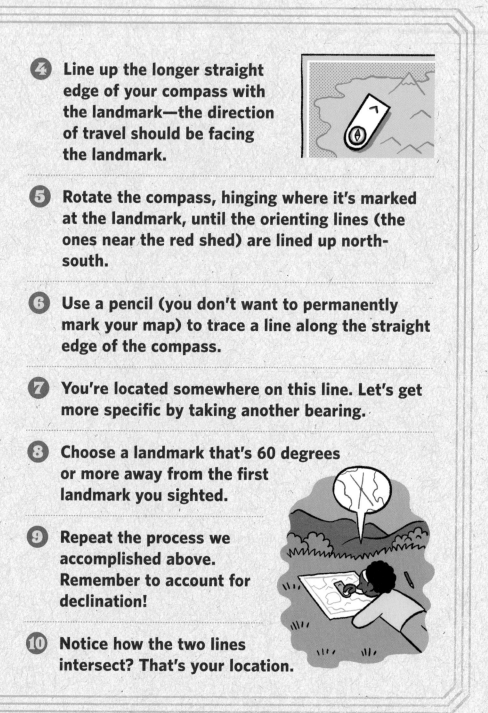

5 Rotate the compass, hinging where it's marked at the landmark, until the orienting lines (the ones near the red shed) are lined up north-south.

6 Use a pencil (you don't want to permanently mark your map) to trace a line along the straight edge of the compass.

7 You're located somewhere on this line. Let's get more specific by taking another bearing.

8 Choose a landmark that's 60 degrees or more away from the first landmark you sighted.

9 Repeat the process we accomplished above. Remember to account for declination!

10 Notice how the two lines intersect? That's your location.

Part 2: Get the Bearing for Your Destination

With your current known location marked on a map, next you'll want to find your intended destination and get there—that's the whole point, right?

1 **Declination time. Make sure it's still set up.**

2 **With your map laid out flat, line up the longer straight edge of your compass with your location.**

3 **Rotate the compass so the same straight edge is now lined up with your destination. Think of moving the compass on the map like it's your known position.**

4 **Make sure the direction of travel arrow is pointed in the direction of your destination and that north on your bezel is pointing to north on the map.**

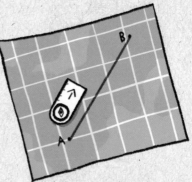

5 Rotate the bezel so that your orienting lines are lined up with north and south on the map.

6 Now check the compass's index line—that's your bearing.

7 Put away your map, stand up, and with the direction of travel arrow facing out, rotate your body around until red is in the shed.

8 You're ready to go. As you walk toward your destination, remember to keep the compass facing the same direction and always make sure red is in the shed.

THE MODERN NAVIGATOR

RADIO WAVES FROM SEA TO SPACE

At just 20 years old, Guglielmo Marconi changed the world forever with the ring of a bell. Working in his parents' attic in Italy, the young inventor created a device that could generate and receive radio waves. By pushing a button on one side of the room, he produced these signals. On the other side of the room a simple antenna picked them up, and with the help of a battery, it rang a bell. It didn't take long for Marconi to expand the possibilities of his newfound technology to navigation and beyond.

Marconi soon moved to England, where the government was interested in supporting his work and where he had spent time as a boy. Four years later, in 1898, Marconi upped the ante, sending a radio signal 18 miles (29km). Then, in 1901, he silenced his naysayers by sending a transmission across the Atlantic Ocean.

Of course, Marconi didn't just invent the radio out of thin air. Like so many innovations in navigation we've looked at, his creation was the result of an exchange of ideas across lands and time.

Radio waves are **electromagnetic energy**—a special type of force composed of a magnetic field (like the one surrounding Earth) interacting with an electric field. Radio waves have high points and low points, just like ocean waves. The number of times a wave rises and falls determines its **frequency**. The higher the

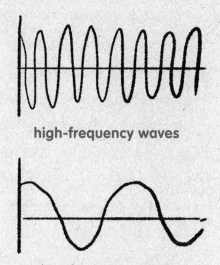

high-frequency waves

low-frequency waves

frequency, the greater the amount of information a radio wave can send. Radio waves can carry everything from simple Morse code to live radio and television broadcasts.

Marconi took the concepts his predecessors developed and ran with them. He invented a **transmitter** to send radio waves and a **receiver** to detect and process these signals. All put together, these components made up the first wireless communication system.

This technology would go on to form the basis for technologies we use every day. From cell phone signals to television to the satellite Global Positioning System (GPS)—which tells us exactly where we are on the earth within just *3 meters*—it all stems from radio waves.

GOING WIRELESS

From the moment wireless communication became possible, the world changed forever. Suddenly the huge distances between continents broke down as barriers for human connection. Messages could be sent far across the planet in real time, with news and music not far behind. Navigators were among the first to adopt the technology and use it to improve their methods of getting around.

For more than a century, sailors had used chronometers to keep time at sea and track their longitude. Even the most accurate lost track of a few seconds on a long trip. Wireless communication allowed navigators to check the accuracy of their chronometers far from port. By the early 1900s, governments from North America and Europe started broadcasting hourly time signals. Ships that had a receiver could set their chronometers to the signal, knowing their watches were on time and their longitude could be measured accurately.

Soon after, a new technology emerged that created a sort of radio compass on board. The **radio direction finder (RDF)**, a device used by ships and aircraft alike, could show navigators where a particular broadcast was coming from. And with that, they could not only determine the direction of the station, but also the location of their ship or airplane using two or more known radio signals.

Early RDF systems actually have a lot in common with the compass. Remember when we learned how to take a bearing and triangulate? The basics of RDF are built on those same ideas. On a ship or aircraft, a navigator would receive a signal via their directional antennae. Based on the strength of the signal, they could tell the direction of where the station was broadcasting from. The navigator could then set a bearing accordingly. This is how radio transmitters got the name "radio beacon."

boat

radio
station

radio
station

For even more precise navigation, pilots caught waves from two or more stations. Then they could use the same technique we learned with our compass: triangulation. Navigators plotted the lines of the location of those stations to find their own location.

Radio navigation technology advanced quickly through the 1920s. It allowed for the safe and effective travel of ships and airplanes. Manufacturing was taking off too, making goods like radios cheaper and more accessible to the masses. Development sped up even more at the end of the 1930s when World War II broke out in Europe.

Both sides of the war put everything they had into out-navigating the other side by utilizing radio waves. RDF technology got smaller, more accurate, and easier to conceal. Around this time, another technology arose that applied radio waves in a different way: radar.

EARLY RADIO TRANSMISSIONS SAVE LIVES

In the early hours of April 15, 1912, one of history's deadliest recorded maritime disasters took place when the RMS *Titanic* struck an iceberg. There weren't enough lifeboats on board, and more than 1,500 people were claimed by the sea. The 705 passengers who survived had one radio to thank.

Distress calls from the doomed ship reached other nearby vessels that came to the survivors' aid. Without radio technology, they would have been stranded in the frigid North Atlantic waters. Guglielmo Marconi himself was scheduled to be on the *Titanic*, but he had hopped on the *Lusitania* a month earlier.

The Wide World of Radar

Radar technology extends far beyond communication and navigation. From everyday energy saving to peering into the earth's core, here are just a few of the ways that radar influences how we live.

AUTOMATIC DOORS AND LIGHTS: We have radar to thank for doors that open just by walking up to them and lights that blink on when they sense movement. Their tiny sensors aren't only convenient, they can save a lot of energy.

WEATHER TRACKING: If you've ever watched a weather report, you've probably heard of Doppler radar. This technology tracks precipitation and storms, helping us keep safe and dry by giving advance warning of when and how hard bad weather will hit.

MEDICAL DIAGNOSTICS: Radar is even used at the doctor's office. Scanning parts of the body using radar technology helps doctors make a diagnosis without the need for surgery.

WILDLIFE CONSERVATION: Scientists use radar to track populations of animals as they migrate. They can then determine any new patterns of movement and find out if a species is in danger.

AGRICULTURE: Farmers use earth-penetrating radar to test the mineral and water content of soil and check on the health of their crops before they even sprout.

GEOLOGY: Now scientists employ high-tech radar to study the movements of 62-mile (100km) thick slabs of the earth's crust. Radar can even detect early warning signs of a volcano that's about to erupt.

SEA ICE MONITORING: Together, the massive sheets of sea ice around the poles are more than three times the size of Australia and help moderate Earth's climate. Radar is a key tool in tracking the melting of sea ice.

RADAR: SEEING THROUGH THE AIRWAVES

Like scuba, lasers, and everyone's favorite canned meat, Spam, **radar** is an abbreviation or acronym. (By the way, it's believed that Spam stands for Special Processed American Meat. Yum?) Well, radar is really a loose acronym from Radio Detection and Ranging. It uses radio waves to detect the location and position of everything from ships to weather.

Radar works a lot like echoes. If you shout in the middle of a field, you won't hear any echo. If you shout against a tall wall, however, the sound waves come right back to you. With radar, a broadcaster transmits radio waves and listens for the signal to bounce back to them.

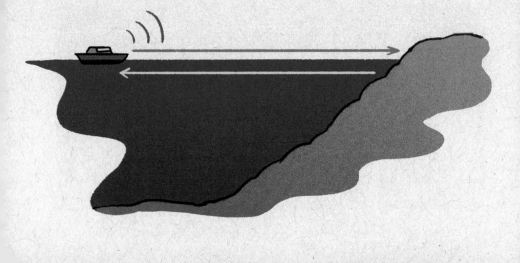

A ship could send out its own radar signal to detect land, obstacles (like reefs), or other ships. Or if you're a modern-day fisherman, you might use radar to detect fish near your boat.

Users send a mix of different frequency signals depending on what they are trying to detect. Lower-frequency radar can broadcast signals a long distance or detect objects that are so far away they appear below the horizon. Higher-frequency radar can't travel as far but offers a more specific directional signal. For instance, low-frequency might tell a plane where a faraway country is, while high-frequency could show it the airport to land in.

Radio navigation saw some big advancements up in the cockpit as well. Higher frequencies offered stronger signals. A greater network of beacons meant easier navigation and safer flying.

Suddenly flying across great distances in rough weather wasn't such a big deal with radio instruments there to guide pilots. The introduction of Very High Frequency Omnidirectional Radio Range (VOR) in the 1950s meant that pilots got better accuracy, but there was a need for more beacons.

There are now more than 3,000 VOR stations around the world, though these are gradually being phased out in favor of satellite navigation. The stations, which sort of look like a sombrero the size of a house, send out two signals. First there's the general blast that goes out in all directions. Then there's a second signal that's released in bursts, focusing on different directions around 360 degrees. The two signals are compared on board an aircraft to determine direction.

Flying with VOR is sort of like crossing a creek by hopping along rocks. Pilots check their charts to see which station to tune into in their area. As they fly farther from that station, they tune into the next one. This continues until they've reached their destination. Along the way, pilots follow a compass-like instrument called an **omni bearing indicator** that tells them how far they are from the signal. As long as the pilot can get a signal from the station, they'll know they're on the correct course.

THE GYROSCOPE: POWERING ROCKETS AND AUTOPILOT

Could something as simple as a spinning toy top hold the key to rocket science and the next innovation in navigation? Well, sort of. **Gyroscopes** are like the fancy, scientific version of a spinning top. They are composed of a spinning wheel with an axis line that goes through the middle of it. Then there are two or three supports around it called gimbals. When the wheel is spinning,

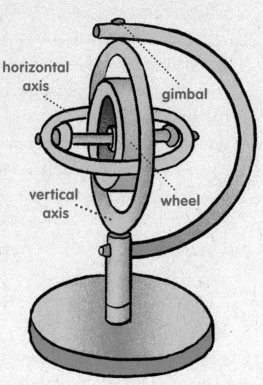

horizontal axis

gimbal

vertical axis

wheel

it always remains stable and any force that tries to mess with it is met with a counterforce.

The name was coined by physicist Jean-Bernard-Léon Foucault in the 1850s. Foucault used gyroscopes to illustrate the earth's ability to remain spinning on its axis. The gyroscope's amazing stability later caught the eye of navigators.

So how have pilots put these gadgets to good use? Gyroscopes were combined with accelerometers (which measure changes in speed) and basic computers to create **inertial navigation systems**. Inside one, the gyroscope spins along as usual, even when the plane turns, dips, or changes speed. The gyroscope will still spin steadily, while its gimbals detect the change made by the plane. A sensor in the gimbals then sends a message to the plane's onboard computer and pilot. These systems constantly determine dead reckoning by measuring distance and the plane's direction.

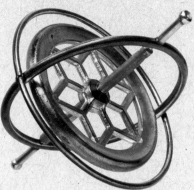

The most basic versions first appeared in rockets during World War II. Not long after, the same technology was adapted to air and sea travel, improving on previous mechanical autopilot systems.

That means that in less than 60 years, we humans went from setting our watches at sea by radio signals to self-piloting rockets and planes. Inertial navigation systems would inspire space programs to reach the next major breakthrough in getting around: satellites.

EARTH'S INCREASINGLY CROWDED ORBIT

If the history of navigation has taught us anything, it's that a device doesn't need to be big to change the world forever. Introducing the **satellite**: an object that orbits (travels around) a bigger object, like a planet.

The first-ever orbiting satellite, *Sputnik 1*, was about the size of a beach ball, but it captivated the entire world. Following World War II, the United States and Soviet Union (today's Russia) were former allies engaged in the Cold War—a tense rivalry to gain power and influence throughout the world. Though America's economy was booming, its space program was just starting up.

The United States had little knowledge of what the Soviet Union was capable of in space. So, when the Soviets launched *Sputnik 1* on October 4, 1957, it caught the world by surprise. The so-called Space Race was on.

Just under four months later, the United States responded with the launch of its first satellite, *Explorer 1*. Meanwhile, the Soviet Union continued reaching new milestones in space. In 1961, they launched the first man (Yuri Gagarin) and, in 1963, the first woman (Valentina Tereshkova) into orbit, who both landed safely back on Earth. Since then, more than 8,300 objects have been launched into space.

Today there are about 5,000 satellites orbiting the earth, but fewer than half of them are actively sending and receiving signals. Then there are the millions of pieces of space debris (also known as space junk)—bits of old rockets, satellites, and spare space station parts that have smashed into each other and are locked in the earth's orbit. But don't worry, someone is starting to clean it up. In 2018, a British university launched a satellite whose only mission is tidying up the outer atmosphere.

We use satellites for everything from photographing the outer reaches of the universe (shout-out to the Hubble Space Telescope), to beaming soccer matches onto screens around the world, to checking up on the weather. A few lucky people even live on one satellite, the International Space Station, which has been in orbit since 1998. And of course, there are the specially designed navigation satellites that are the pinnacle of human achievement when it comes to getting around.

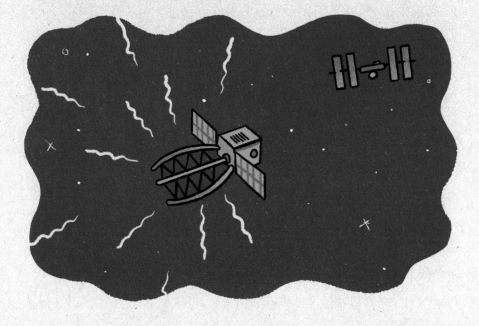

GO SATELLITE-GAZING

We know the benefits of getting familiar with the stars, but there's a lot more up there than those distant masses of burning gas. Satellites are a reminder of the astonishing things humans can do with some scientific know-how. From anywhere you can see stars, you can see satellites. Here are a few tips to get you started.

1. Go out on a clear night with a new moon (that's when the moon is barely visible)—you'll get the best look at the night sky then. (You can use a lunar calendar in an almanac or online to help you find a new moon.)

2. Spot the difference between a plane and a satellite. Planes blink as they fly across the sky and flash blue or red navigation lights. Satellites rarely blink and appear white in the sky.

3. Notice how different satellites have varying speeds and orbital paths.

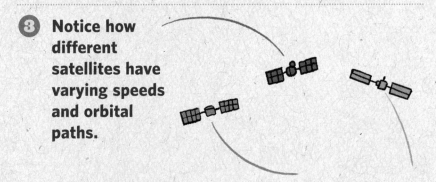

4. There are many resources that offer live tracking of satellites. The website maps.esri.com/rc/sat2 offers a free live map of satellites orbiting the earth. They're labeled by purpose (like navigation, communication, or weather) and the site lists their launch date, country of origin, and orbit path. You can also track the paths of some of the famous ones, like the International Space Station and Hubble Space Telescope.

SATELLITE NAVIGATION: FROM MISSILES TO MAPPING YOUR HIKE

As humans, we've gone from looking to the stars for answers to looking somewhere much closer: Earth's outer atmosphere. Navigation satellites whip around our planet some 12,400 miles (19,956km) above sea level. They give us answers about our location that would absolutely astound early navigators. These satellites provide location data accurate up to 10 feet (3m). Satellite navigation uses the same basic principles as radio navigation, but that's where the similarities end. We're in all new territory.

Today we use the term GPS to describe any satellite navigation, but GPS (originally called Navstar) is really just one network of satellites. Since GPS is the first and most widely used, we'll explore that one in detail.

Like radio navigation, GPS has its roots in war. It was born out of the same Space Race that gave us the speedy adoption (and launches) of early satellites. GPS was originally developed to increase the United States Air Force's missile accuracy. The first GPS satellite launched in 1978, and 10 more would be in orbit by 1985. Eventually the system would contain a total of 24 satellites orbiting Earth.

Get to Know Coordinates

GPS coordinates tell you your precise location of latitude and longitude. They are written as a set of two numbers with a positive or negative value or a cardinal direction (N, E, S, or W). For instance, Chicago is either: 41.8781°, -87.6298° or N 41.8781°, W 87.6298°.

Positive latitude coordinates refer to latitudes north of the equator. Negative latitudes are south of the equator. Meanwhile, positive longitude coordinates are east of the prime meridian, and negative longitudes are west of the prime meridian.

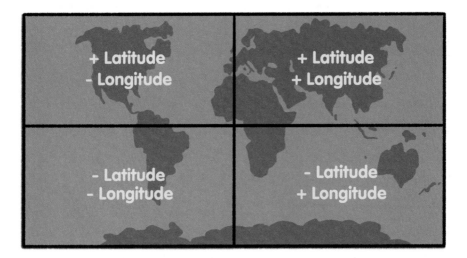

+ Latitude
- Longitude

+ Latitude
+ Longitude

- Latitude
- Longitude

- Latitude
+ Longitude

Originally the US government had no plans of making GPS available to the public. Everything changed in 1983, however, after a Korean passenger jet drifted off its flight path and was shot down in Soviet airspace. The tragedy was a wake-up call for US officials. They realized that GPS had the potential to make air travel much safer and made GPS available to the public—well, sort of. They reserved the best signals for military use, making the civilian service unreliable and ineffective.

The original GPS receiver for the general public hit the market in 1989. The Magellan Nav-1000 cost $3,000 and was created with boaters and backcountry hikers in mind. It looked like a brick crossed with a calculator. The reviews were not favorable, but the technology was still exciting.

It wasn't until 2000 that the US government opened up GPS altogether. That meant free, full signals for anyone anywhere in the world (with a few hard-to-reach exceptions, of course). The receivers got cheaper, and the signals got much stronger. With better technology, the applications for everyday people grew to include driving navigation.

MORE THAN DIRECTIONS

The possibilities for GPS extend far beyond navigation to just about every aspect of daily life. The farmers who grew the food you ate today likely used GPS to plan a more efficient harvest by tracking when certain crops are at their peak. Your favorite athletes utilize GPS to maximize their training by tracking speed and distance. Self-driving cars, environmental conservationists, sneaker sellers, fishermen—all of them and more benefit from GPS technology!

A Coordinated Effort

HOW GPS WORKS

To understand GPS, it's easiest to think of it in three segments: space, the user, and control.

The space segment is where you'll find the satellites. GPS has 24 satellites whipping around the earth in a carefully choreographed dance. Think of them like moving flashlights, but instead of projecting light they are sending signals. GPS reaches practically every inch of the earth's surface (except for some nooks and crannies between mountains) thanks to the satellites' constant orbit. At any time, at least four GPS satellites are observing any bit of the earth's surface.

Then there's the user. The user's GPS device (like a smartphone or smartwatch) receives the signals from a group of four satellites. Note that the user doesn't send any data back to the GPS—the device only gathers a signal. Here's why four or more satellites are needed for one position: At least three satellites are required to triangulate the user's coordinate positions, just like how airplanes use radio triangulation. Then another corrects for any time differences in the signals.

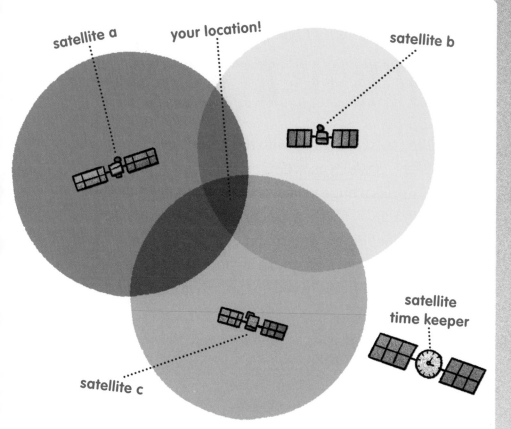

satellite a

your location!

satellite b

satellite time keeper

satellite c

What if the satellites get thrown into an irregular orbit? That's what the <u>control</u> is for. Monitoring stations around the world gather data from the satellites as they pass while ground antennae relay commands. A master control station in Colorado acts as the brain of the system. All these units work together to make sure the satellites are showing up right on time for their 12-hour orbit of Earth.

FIND YOUR GPS COORDINATES

AND SEARCH FOR TREASURE

Let's go treasure hunting with the help of satellites. Geocaching, which uses GPS coordinates to find hidden treasure, has a huge following around the world. It's an outdoor activity where amateur adventurers share the GPS coordinates for waterproof boxes (called caches) that contain little prizes and a logbook so you can see who found the cache before you. In this activity, you'll get a feel for geocaching.

SUPPLIES NEEDED: a friend, two adults, a park or outdoor area you can roam safely, two smartphones or GPS devices, two notebooks and two pencils, and two pieces of treasure (something bright and colorful, at least the size of a soccer ball).

1 Have you and your friend split up into two groups. Each group should have an adult, a GPS device, a notebook and pen, and treasure!

2 Start by hiding your treasure somewhere in the park or outdoor zone. Don't bury it or make it too hard to see—at least for the first few rounds.

3 In your notebook, write down the GPS coordinates of the place where you left the treasure. (In a smartphone, you can find this by tapping and holding your location in Google Maps.) Write down the coordinates. They should look something like this: 41.076806, -71.895053.

4 Meet up with the other treasure hunting team and exchange written coordinates. Enter their written coordinates into your device—be sure to type in every digit! The more precise the coordinates are, the closer you'll get to the treasure.

5 As you walk, keep an eye on how the GPS is measuring your speed. If you slow down the pace, how does the GPS react?

6 Collect your treasure! Did the coordinates lead you right to the bounty?

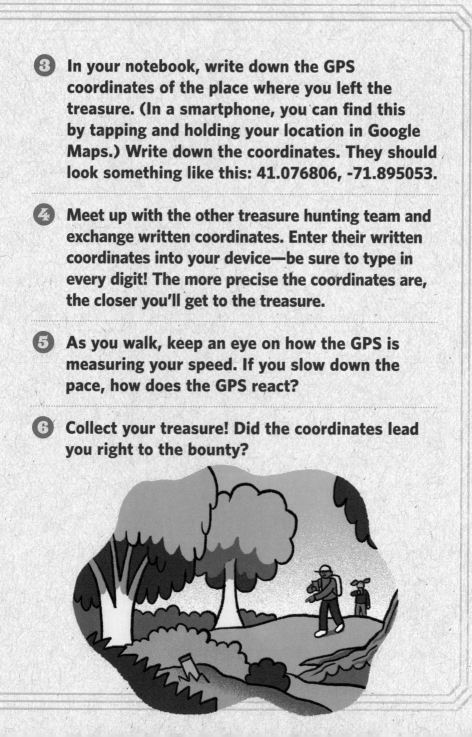

THE GOOD AND THE BAD OF GPS

GPS represents a remarkable breakthrough for navigation. Not only can we easily find our exact position anywhere on Earth, we can mark it, plan a route back, and even know when we will arrive. Measuring distance, speed, and direction—GPS ticks all the boxes a navigator needs. It's so easy to use that you can just punch in a direction and it tells you right where to go and for how long. You don't even need to look up from the screen! And that is one of the major downsides to GPS, too.

GPS receivers can get lost, broken, or run out of electrical charge. You might even find yourself in one of those rare places between mountain peaks or underground where the signals are weak. Reliance on this one tool alone is a recipe for failure.

Every one of navigation's many innovations and technologies—whether it's a stick chart, sextant, or satellite—builds off a deep knowledge of what came before it. When a new invention comes along, it doesn't mean the tools that preceded it are no longer useful. It simply means we have another option.

GPS makes it hard to get lost—and no doubt that's a good thing. When the weather gets rough and the terrain is unfamiliar, the guidance of a satellite is always welcome. But the signals might not always come in. The airwaves could go silent. Our batteries might die, or our receiver might get soaked. That's why we read coordinates as well as stars. Knowledge about all forms of navigation gives us the confidence to move around this crazy planet, knowing that we can go anywhere and truly not get lost.

AFTERWORD

★ ★ ★

You've made it this far in the journey—congratulations! Pat yourself on the back (go ahead, do it) and take a look outside. Do you see what's around you differently than when you started this book? Does the angle of the sun give you a clue as to the time of day or direction you're facing? Are the trees a path to north or south? Do the stars provide a compass? I hope the answer is yes.

Observation is at the heart of the many skills, tools, and techniques we've covered in this book. From the earliest human star navigators to the modern satellites high above, what they all have in common is a discerning eye on the world around us. As you explore the planet with the knowledge gained from this book, remember that observation is the best tool you'll ever have. You can't forget it at home, it doesn't break, and

no one can ever take it away from you. Watching the world around you with a knowing eye will inspire confidence to venture further and seek out new places to see, people to meet, and experiences that you'll never forget.

The curiosity that led you to pick up this book is part of the same spark of adventure that led early navigators to set out beyond the horizon. The desire to learn is a key part of what makes us human. Feeding that desire connects us to the generations of people that came before us and deepens our connection to our own communities. When those ideas are shared and spread to new people and places, they evolve.

So explore with confidence. Share what you know. Keep your mind open and remember that learning is the greatest adventure you'll ever set out on. And it's a journey that will never end.

FURTHER READING

★ ★ ★

BOOKS

Explorers: Amazing Tales of the World's Greatest Adventures by Nellie Huang

What We See in the Stars: An Illustrated Tour of the Night Sky by Kelsey Oseid

Maps of the World: An Illustrated Children's Atlas of Adventure, Culture, and Discovery by Enrico Lavagno

Children's Illustrated Atlas from DK and the Smithsonian

ONLINE RESOURCES

timeandnavigation.si.edu

Looking for a comprehensive online guide to all forms of navigation? This Smithsonian Institution site features detailed histories and tons of new activities to test your knowledge.

timeanddate.com/astronomy

Need to know solar noon or looking for information on an upcoming eclipse? Time and Date has up-to-the-minute info on the position of the sun, stars, and moon in your area.

hokulea.com

The homepage of the Polynesian Voyaging Society contains a history of traditional wayfinding and updates on the journeys of voyaging canoes at sea.

whose.land

How well do you know the history of where you live? Whose Land is an interactive map that shows the Indigenous territory for places around the world.

rmg.co.uk/discover

Home to the prime meridian, the Royal Museums Greenwich site offers great nautical navigation history with special attention to the history of longitude.

usgs.gov

Interested in maps and how they're used? The United States Geological Survey site features constantly updating maps of the country's natural resources and natural hazards like earthquakes and volcanoes.

ngdc.noaa.gov/geomag/declination.shtml

We know the earth's magnetic field is always changing. The National Centers for Environmental Information site offers an easy and fun tool for tracking it. Find out the declination for any coordinates in the world.

ACKNOWLEDGMENTS

★ ★ ★

This book would not be possible without the hard work and dedication of many people around the world. First and foremost, I owe endless gratitude to the team at Workman for believing in me as a writer and giving me the pages to explore this topic and share it with a new generation of adventurers. I'd especially like to acknowledge my editor, Danny Cooper, whose attention to detail and genuine interest in even the most obscure of subjects inspired me to dig deeper into navigation.

Illustrations play a key role in this book, and few artists could have brought this subject to life quite like Andrés Lozano. At Workman, thank you to Sara Corbett, Christine Kettner, Angie Chen, Hillary Leary, Abigail Sokolsky, Cindy Lee, and Emily Weldon for helping create and share the story in this book.

My interest in navigation was born out of my time in the outdoors. Growing up, I had open access to the shores of the Great Lakes and the dense forests of Northern Michigan's Upper Peninsula on the traditional land of the Omāēqnomenew (Menominee) people and Sault Tribe of Chippewa Indians. My parents equipped me with basic outdoor and water safety knowledge, then left me to wander and explore. This time in the outdoors shaped who I am. I am indebted to the people who came before me and those who will come after me who continue to advocate for public access to the outdoors.

The journey of creating this book started in Hawai'i with the

Polynesian Voyaging Society, where I was working on a story for a national magazine. I'd like to thank my editor (and fellow adventure enthusiast) Will Grant for believing in the power of that story. I'd also like to thank Polynesian Voyaging Society crewmembers Austin Kino and Archie Kalepa who opened their world to me and made me feel welcome in their community. I would also like to thank Nainoa Thompson, president of the Polynesian Voyaging Society, for penning the foreword for this story and for his dedication to spreading navigation knowledge to new generations of explorers around the world. Nainoa embodies the spirit of learning and serves as a continual inspiration to me.

Learning is a journey that should never end. Without teachers (and the teachers of my teachers) this book would not be possible. I am fortunate to have had teachers that inspired me to continue learning outside of the classroom and to believe in myself. My first memory of really loving school is when my fifth grade teacher, Joy Peterich, encouraged my class to question what was written in our textbooks. Sometimes we find teachers later in life that we never even get to meet. Wayne Campbell and his commitment to education through videos helped immensely with the writing of this book. His curiosity about the world was contagious.

Writing can sometimes feel solitary, but luckily I had company along the way. My trusty dog, Goji, curled up beneath my desk on cold, snowy mornings and balmy summer nights while writing this book, reminded me to take a break and head out for a walk when I was stumped. This book truly would not be possible without the love and support of my wife, Amanda. No doubt my biggest supporter and adventure-buddy, she also pored over early pages with a keen eye. Here's to the next adventure together.

INDEX

★ ★ ★

Hans Aschim lives in Brooklyn, New York, with his wife and their dog, Goji. On weekends, you can find him out on mini-adventures in the Catskill Mountains or in the waters off of Rockaway Beach.

Andrés Lozano is a Madrid-born and London-based artist. He divides his time between illustration and painting. He has also co-authored several picture books originally published in the UK and the US and now translated to more than ten languages.

Nainoa Thompson is president of the Polynesian Voyaging Society and a Pwo navigator. He is the recipient of the National Geographic Society's Hubbard Medal and the Explorers Club Medal.

★ ★ ★